Reza de Wet

PLAYS TWO
AFRICAN GOTHIC
GOOD HEAVENS
BREATHING IN

Introduction by Marthinus Basson

OBERON BOOKS
LONDON

First published in English in 2005 by Oberon Books Ltd.
(incorporating Absolute Classics)
521 Caledonian Road, London N7 9RH
Tel: 020 7607 3637 / Fax: 020 7607 3629
e-mail: oberon.books@btinternet.com
www.oberonbooks.com

A catalogue record for this book is available from the British Library.

ISBN: 1 84002 480 1

Cover illustration: Andrzej Klimowski

Printed in Great Britain by Antony Rowe Ltd, Chippenham.

To Marthinus Basson for bringing my plays alive
with such immaculate artistry

And to my distinguished agent and friend
Gordon Dickerson who has with unfailing
support and encouragement made this collection
possible

My sincere thanks to Ann Haywood and Dan Steward for their patient and meticulous work on these texts.

Contents

Introduction

In 1985 when playwright Reza de Wet unleashed her creative vision, fully formed and perfectly pitched, on an unsuspecting and quite impotent South African theatre scene, she presented a subtle but radical alternative to the agitprop and comfortable entertainment seen on our stages at that time. Right from the beginning of what has become a sustained and prolific career, she proved to be able to unnerve and amuse in equal measure while tapping into a dark and richly subversive vein, mining both gold and puss from a festering Afrikaner psyche.

South Africa then, of course, was a very different place from the country we know today.

Black schoolchildren were marching in the streets, protesting against a repressive system of Apartheid and a second-rate education in Afrikaans (then called 'the Language of the Oppressor'). The police were shooting at these children. Young white men, on the other hand, were expected to pass into manhood and citizenship by a two-year rite of passage, fighting a senseless and indefensible terrorist war on our borders. Mothers organised knitting circles to make socks for their sons and sent Christmas parcels (that invariably contained rusks and a Bible) to a mysterious 'front' somewhere up north. The State-controlled radio and television quite successfully fed us a sanitized version of the truth, and from the pulpits of the Dutch Reformed Church religious leaders extolled the Nationalists' version of 'loving thy neighbour as thyself' in the comforting guise of 'separate but equal'.

And apart from the occasional bump up against reality, we could still pretend that the world we lived in was relatively safe, sound and maybe even moral.

Censorship was the order of the day. I will never forget the combination of utter thrill and total panic when, returning from a first visit to Europe, I succeeded in smuggling a copy of Jean Genet's novel *The Thief's Journal* through customs, a small nondescript act of rebellion in the name of literary enlightenment that could have had rather nasty repercussions. But by 1985 one of the great Afrikaans playwrights, Bartho Smit, had effectively been silenced, and the work of another important playwright, Pieter Fourie, was constantly being emasculated. For a time he was reduced to writing farces.

Censorship, by nature, is insidious and manifests itself in a myriad of small but telling signs: the way one did not engage with a waiter, for example, perhaps from a sense of guilt, perhaps because we were trained not to acknowledge our fellow, second-class citizens as human. Or the way friends from differing race groups unquestioningly separated at the station entrance only to meet up on the same platform to continue a conversation and separate again when entering the train. We were effectively trained to become censors ourselves and so avoid asking the questions that could make it difficult not to act on the information that we grew to ignore.

Though there was a very active and vocal resistance movement on South African stages at the time, notably at The Space Theatre in Cape Town and The Market Theatre in Johannesburg, most of the older generation of worthwhile Afrikaans dramatists who had been opposing the status quo since the early days of Apartheid had given up writing for the stage or were lured away by the financial benefits of television. The desperately needed voice of resistance from within was particularly absent. Working as a young director in a State-subsidized theatre, I had to turn to the work of, for instance, the German playwright Heiner Müller, to find the potent metaphors with which to address the rot in our society.

To counter the drought that hit Afrikaans drama, the Afrikaans Language and Culture Organization (ATKV) started an annual Campus Festival to stimulate new student drama, and it is here that Reza, the actress born in the small town of Senekal in the Free State, now Assistant Professor in the Drama Department at Rhodes University in Grahamstown, staged her first play. From this debut it was immediately clear that a major new voice had announced itself.

African Gothic (*Diepe Grond*, 1985) understandably sparked off intense debate. Using a technique of literary model or reference that has served Reza de Wet well over the years (an entire thesis could be constructed around her use of fairy-tales, Christian myth and references to the works of Poe, the Brontës and obviously Chekhov) *African Gothic* was a knowing subversion of a popular Afrikaans children's story set on an idyllic farm; a South African Eden where the parents were good and responsible, the children safe and sound, the black nanny a second mother and friend, the workers smiling and happy and a benevolent God ever-watchful and at home in Heaven.

With one perverse and masterly gesture Reza de Wet killed off the parents who built the world we grew up in and made the brother and sister transgressors of that primal taboo, incest, lovers doomed to re-enact key incidents from their childhood to pass the time. A mainly silent black nanny, who has become both mother and God, watches with great love as her former employer's children self-destruct. Even the order of day and night are reversed. Frikkie and Soekie go to sleep at sunrise and rise at sunset to start their work. Where crops used to grow from neatly ploughed furrows, the farm now lies fallow as they burrow through the floor of their room in a futile attempt to strike a source of life-giving water.

Here was a play that clearly overturned every single rule and moral principle that upheld society and were accepted as the norm by the very people that set up the Campus Festival. I find it ironic that a need for new dramatists in some ways heralded the birth of a new type of Afrikaner. Just a year later the Rock movement know as 'Voëlvry' (meaning: 'to be declared an outlaw') launched itself as a populist form of protest and gave voice to a rebellious generation of Frikkies and Soekies who, through music, happily killed their parents and what they stood for.

The next year she consolidated her reputation at the same festival with the much less angry, but more subtle and charming *Good Heavens* (*Op Dees Aarde*, 1985). This tale, peopled with small-town characters, was, however, no less subversive and introduced some of the enduring themes that run through much of her work. These have come to a shattering head in her most recent play *Breathing In* (2004), set in the last days of the Anglo-Boer War.

My first experience as director of Reza de Wet's work came in about 1993 when I (as resident director) approached her to write a play for the then Cape Performing Arts Board (CAPAB). She was at the time finishing her trilogy *Missing, Miracle* and *Crossing*. She agreed to write a play for us around the lives of Chekhov's *Three Sisters* (set during the last days of the Russian revolution). We presented the trilogy as a season that year, and her *Three Sisters Two* took on an extra meaning when it became the last play to be performed before the CAPAB Drama Department was disbanded in 1995.

Having been fortunate enough to direct quite a number of them, I know that Reza de Wet's plays can seem quite simple and straightforward and could easily be grouped under labels like Fairy-tale, Magic Realism or Post-modern, yet they are unique in many ways and very, very deceptive, in the same way that the reflection of the sky in a pond with floating leaves is a pleasant illusion, masking a rich soup of rotting vegetation or worse. Trust me, it can be home to dangerous little larvae that might burrow into your skin, or host lurking creatures that could drag you down and drown you.

I have always found it thrilling to unravel the little rituals of storytelling and the hidden meanings. For instance, *Missing*'s Afrikaans title, *Mis*, has five meanings: 'mist', 'mass', 'dung', 'to long for' and 'to miss the point or mark', all applicable to the play's themes. Reza de Wet has developed an uncanny way of leading her audience astray by creating a substructure to her plays. This might simultaneously refer to several fairy-tales, or might contain a reference to Greek or Christian myth, but without the reference ever becoming overt or intimidating to her audience. Thus she instills a feeling of curious and non-confrontational familiarity while allowing the true meaning of the piece to seep slowly and unobtrusively through the pores: a slow poison that might kill only days later.

She also employs this form of deception in her choice of setting for her plays. They always take place in the past, creating a comforting place that somehow still feels familiar because it has become part of our fantasy lives or historical past. There, the good seems even better and the bad can be stripped of its immediate horror and threat. She tends to lull her audience into a false sense of security, often by using rhythmical and repetitive patterns of speech with the result that some characters, like Anna in *Breathing In*, attain an almost hypnotic quality. Her use of sayings, metaphors and almost forgotten words, applied with a wicked dose of humour, jolts the collective memory of the audience and sharpens their perception. This use of language, combined with archetypes and even caricatures acting out simple tales constructed around literary models, disguises a vicious and uncompromising analysis of the way we are, have been and will be. It resonates in our subconscious and leaves the audience elated and amused, but also deeply disturbed.

Her characters are well-developed, rich and rounded exercises in stereotypes, archetypes and even caricatures: the spinster, the general, the trickster, the lover, the pretty girl and so forth. And they are very often spectacular liars. Employing the actor's trick of transformation and the intellectual's technique of meta-theatre, she uses the lie to tell a truth much truer that the truth, and so fabricates means of physical or emotional survival when all other means fail.

In *Breathing In* the audience is never sure whether Annie is really fragile, or fragile because her mother would like her, or indeed needs her, to be so. And the fantastical story of Annie's birth: is it true or merely the elaborate fabrication of a serial killer justifying murder?

In *Missing,* when the blind policeman arrives to protect the three women against the abductor of young girls who is loose in town, he tells a moving tale of how he was blinded as a boy by staring into the sun. The tale is filled with sensual detail, highlighting forms of sensory perception other than sight. It also plays with the breaking of taboos and the devastating rewards for this sort of transgression. He is, of course, not blind at all, but the saviour of a repressed young girl, Meisie. He is a clown-like Christ to the father's frightening God. But her salvation by abduction is not necessarily positive. In *Crossing* another trickster, Maestro, has a deeply disturbing and abusive relationship with a similar type of girl, Esmerelda.

South Africa is still a deeply patriarchal society, in spite of major advances in women's rights since the ANC came to power. I would even dare to say that Reza de Wet's entire œuvre is a rebellion against a patriarchal order. Though she is often referred to as a feminist writer, I find that she treats the themes of masculinity and femininity in a much more symbolic and richly psychological fashion than typical feminist literature does. In the absence of men, her women often transform, as some fish do, into a substitute male. And when they do, they take on a lot of the negative qualities traditionally ascribed to the male. She seems to accept that masculinity and femininity make up a solid mandala, doomed to a symbiotic existence for all eternity, and that this relationship, when unbalanced by need, survival or obsessive and destructive romantic love, gives rise to epic and often comic battles of will.

In both *Good Heavens* and *Breathing In* De Wet explores the interdependent, volatile and destructive nature of male and female interaction. She has found some truly novel ways in which to subvert the male principle.

In *Good Heavens* the only male on stage, Tommie, is an undertaker's assistant. His eldest sister is fulfilling the traditional male role of decision-maker in the house, while he, in an apron, helps in the kitchen. His only human contact outside of the family circle is restricted to washing corpses. This, of course, undermines any possibility of either a normal relationship or the continuation of a bloodline. In *Missing* (from her second trilogy) the father of the house has withdrawn to the loft and has been up there for seven years after losing his farm due to the Depression. He never speaks (the silence of God?), but once a day roars his anguish, and in return for the food his loving wife sends up by basket, he rewards her with a pail of urine and excrement.

In *Breathing In* the nameless, wounded General is the potent male, patriarchal and patriotic, but now flat on his back. The herbalist, Anna, is keeping this leader of a beleaguered and ragged band of soldiers fighting a war soon to be lost, in a drugged state. He becomes a blank canvas on which she can project her need and resentment, and he is used as a lure for the young Adjutant Brand, a vital but headless chicken who cannot take a decision without the blessing of his leader. Infirm of purpose, he comes to a sticky end in an uncompromising end-game, orchestrated by

Anna to save her bloodless daughter Annie. Brand, Christ-like, dies so that Annie can live. But he is not resurrected because he lacks the capacity to submit uncompromisingly to the needs of a female. A case of the bridegroom stripped bare.

Reza de Wet's plays, with the exception of her elaborations on the work of Chekhov, are mostly pieces for small sets of individual voices, and are as finely constructed and demanding as good chamber music. It requires great skill from the performer, and in playing, the actor has to be able to strike a fine balance between reality and a sense of poetry, and must skilfully negotiate the tricky corners of humour, tragedy and even melodrama. Her characters, even the nice ones, need an almost feral 'attack'. As director I have been surprised that the scripts stand up very well to being deconstructed, and frankly one of the best performances of her *Yelena* (an elaboration on Chekhov's *Uncle Vanya*) was a re-rehearsal, stripped of set and costumes.

Reza de Wet has never written an overtly political play. She has never explored our contemporary reality from the perspective of a day to day existence, and though I was once told by a German director that he could not see the point of her re-writing Chekhov's *Three Sisters*, he (perhaps understandably) missed the fact that it was a direct comment on the end of Afrikaner rule in South Africa.

The Afrikaner is a contradictory creature. We have a complex and difficult history of abusing, and being abused, and it clings to us like a hump. We were taught by the system we created to think around corners whilst trying to shoot straight from the hip. For me Reza de Wet's work will always be quality, hand-crafted lace that shows much beauty while it exposes a potent sweat of guilt and the power of raw muscle.

Marthinus Basson, Stellenbosch 2004

Marthinus Basson, widely regarded as the foremost South African director, is particularly known for his visionary and eclectic productions which consistently extend the boundaries of South African theatre. He has directed nine Reza de Wet texts, for which he has received numerous nominations and awards as director and designer.

AFRICAN GOTHIC

Characters

SUSSIE

thirty-four, a child-woman who combines a naive spontaneity with an over-ripe sensuality. When – as indicated in the text – she speaks in a *child voice*, she becomes an innocent six year-old child. However, when the *mother's voice* is indicated, she adopts the persona of her stern and puritanical mother. She does not play these different parts, but rather becomes them

FRIKKIE

thirty, her brother. There is a dangerous, predatory quality about him, except when he adopts the role of the shy and gauche *young boy* or assumes a harsh *father's voice*

ALINA

sixty, their black nanny. She exudes an almost numinous power and all her actions speak of a quiet and assured dignity

GROVÉ

thirty-five, a lawyer from Bloemfontein. He is pale, balding and wears glasses. He is neatly dressed and speaks in a controlled and precise manner

Accent

These characters are not English-speaking South Africans, but Afrikaners and as such a 'South African' accent is not required. 'Normal' English can be used, since the convention is that the characters are speaking Afrikaans.

The original Afrikaans version of this play, *Diepe Grond*, was first staged in 1985 by the ATKV in the Breytenbach Theatre in Pretoria, and was directed by Denys Webb. The first professional production of this play was staged in 1986 by The Market Theatre in Johannesburg, and was directed by Lucille Gillwald.

This English language version was first produced at the Kwasuka Theatre, Durban, South Africa by Art for Africa, on 6 June 2003, with the following cast:

FRIKKIE, Steven Stead

SUSSIE, Belinda Harwood

GROVÉ, Frantz Dobrowsky

ALINA, Patti Nokwe

Designed and Directed by Greg King

Thanks to Denys Webb and the ATKV, to Mannie Manim and The Market Theatre, and to Lucille Gillwald for giving this play such outstanding first productions.

Set

A fly-ridden, decaying farmhouse on a Free State farm. The remnants of a former grandeur serve only as a reminder of better times. At the back there is a passage which runs the entire breadth of the set and forms the *upper level*. Three doors lead off from this area. The floor, centre back, leads to the rest of the house. It is boarded up. Hanging from nails in the door are a 'khaki' hat, a man's hat, a sjambok (short whip) and a catapult (sling). The front door is on the extreme left and the kitchen door is on the extreme right. The kitchen door remains open throughout the play and a section of the kitchen can be seen. The door to the wash-room is front left. In the centre of this upper area there is a large mound of earth with a pitch-handle protruding from it.

All the furniture is on the *lower level* which comprises three quarters of the acting space. Front left there is a window.

There is a copper-and-iron double-bed, left centre, angled from left to right with a night table next to it. There is a soap-box downstage, next to the bed. Against the head of the bed, the side of the bed closest to the audience, is a wooden chest (kist) with enough acting space between the chest and the 'window'.

Front, in the middle, there are two battered Victorian chairs and a round table. Right, slightly to the back, there is a bench with slatted back and sides.

Sound Effects are very important, since this play relies heavily on spirit of place.

The monotonous clacking of a windmill can be heard from time to time throughout the play. At the start of the play the clucking of a few farm chickens can be heard. As it becomes evening, the chicken noises are replaced by the night sounds of Africa, particularly the howling of jackals.

ACT ONE

At the start of the play, the clacking of the windmill can be heard and – from time to time – the clucking of chickens. The interior is dimly lit and bars of light shine through the 'window' and the cracks in the walls. FRIKKIE and SUSSIE are sleeping on the bed. There is the loud sound of the wood-stove in the kitchen being stoked. SUSSIE moans and scratches and huddles close to FRIKKIE. From the kitchen the sound of cups being arranged on a tray. All the while ALINA is singing an hypnotic Sotho song. She continues to sing while SUSSIE wakes up. She yawns, stretches, scratches and sits up slowly. She is wearing a tattered nightgown and there is mud on her legs and feet. She looks under the bed and when she finds the chamber-pot she takes it out from under the bed, lifts her nightgown, sits on it facing the audience and urinates loudly with a look of profound relief on her face.

FRIKKIE: Why do you make such a noise when you pee pee, man?

SUSSIE: (*With her eyes closed.*) Ssht. I'm still sleeping. I'm dreaming.

FRIKKIE: Did the fleas bite you too? (*Scratches.*) I wish we had khaki weed to put under the mattress. But that doesn't even grow any more.

SUSSIE: Don't talk… (*Gets up and pushes the chamber-pot back under the bed.*) Don't talk… (*Gets back into bed.*) Close your eyes. (*Snuggles up to FRIKKIE.*)

FRIKKIE: No. I must get up.

SUSSIE: Please. Just lie a bit. Until old Alina calls us.

FRIKKIE: Not today. I've got things to do. (*Tries to sit up.*)

SUSSIE: (*Pulling him down.*) Don't move. (*Wraps her arms around him.*)

FRIKKIE: You're hurting me.

SUSSIE: (*Loud whisper.*) You must lie very still (*Turns FRIKKIE's head towards her.*) and you must look at me.

FRIKKIE: I don't have time for this.

SUSSIE: I want you to lie quietly. If you move…I'll be angry.

FRIKKIE: Stop it, Sussie.

SUSSIE: Don't talk. You mustn't.

(*FRIKKIE wriggles but SUSSIE holds him down.*)

If you're good…I'll tell you a story about what used to be.

FRIKKIE: I know all your stories.

SUSSIE: Not this one. I promise. I've just remembered it.

FRIKKIE: I don't know…

SUSSIE: You'll like it.

FRIKKIE: I've never heard it?

SUSSIE: Never. (*She lies close to him while she tells the story.*)

I was quite little. The dahlias were high above my head. It was a hot day. I was playing with my doll under the tree.

FRIKKIE: Was it before I was born?

SUSSIE: No. You were somewhere. Ssht. You'll see. Then I heard the garden gate opening and there was Pa. Wearing his khaki clothes and his hat. And then he came and lifted me high up. He called me his little doll and put me on his shoulders. And I could see everything.

FRIKKIE: What did you see?

SUSSIE: I could see the green lucerne and the cowshed and the dam.

FRIKKIE: Was there water in the dam?

SUSSIE: Yes. It was full. I could see the water shining.

FRIKKIE: And the John Deer tractor?

SUSSIE: Yes. It was far away. It looked so small. Like a toy. He wanted to show me something. But then Ma called. She was calling Pa. She was standing on the steps wearing her apron. She said it was hot and we must have something to drink. She held open the screen door and Pa said 'mind your head' and we went in. Inside it was dark. The shutters were closed and the curtains. It didn't smell very nice. I could tell there was tripe cooking on the stove. We went to the dining room and Ma gave us ginger beer. Pa put me on his knee. When he drank his ginger beer, I could hear him swallowing…very loudly. (*Short pause.*) Ma was swotting flies. She swot some on the table. I turned my head and looked at that dark corner between the door and the dresser. And then…I saw him.

FRIKKIE: Who?

SUSSIE: You. I saw you.

FRIKKIE: (*Anxious.*) Why didn't you say that? Why did you call me…'him' like that?

SUSSIE: Ag, I don't know. You were…crouching there… looking at Pa. Your eyes were big…and shining. Ma and Pa didn't see you. You were just sitting there. Not moving. Just sitting there…and looking.

FRIKKIE: I can't remember. (*Sitting up.*) It's a stupid story.

SUSSIE: I can tell you another one.

FRIKKIE: (*Gets up. Very angry.*) Sometimes I think you just …make it up! How can I…find out…if you lie to me?

SUSSIE: I'll never lie to you, Boetie[1]. Cross my heart and hope to die.

(*FRIKKIE crosses to the washroom where he can be heard splashing his face. He is wearing a vest and faded shorts. There is mud on his feet and on his legs.*)

Don't be angry with me! Please! I can tell you something else! Or if you want to…we can play!

FRIKKIE: (*Emerging from the washroom. While he dries his face on his forearm.*) Yes, maybe we can! Maybe we can. Maybe we can play 'Sussie is still sleeping and Ma comes down the passage'.

SUSSIE: (*Quietly.*) No, please not that.

FRIKKIE: Yes! Ma comes down the passage. She walks quietly. You can't hear her but you know she's there. Even in your sleep. You dream…about her getting closer.

SUSSIE: (*Burying her face in the pillow.*) I…don't want to.

FRIKKIE: She stands in the doorway and looks at you. In your dream…her eyes are very big and they burn right through you. She's looking to see…if your hands are where they should be. Folded together…and above the sheet.

(*SUSSIE starts crying softly.*)

Don't cry. Don't cry! Why must you always cry?

(*Old ALINA enters. She is carrying two cups on a tray.*)

---

1 An Afrikaans term of endearment, literally meaning 'little brother'. At times Sussie uses an abbreviated version.

ALINA: Basie[2], Nonnie[3], I see someone is coming. (*Points to the window.*) That side.

(*FRIKKIE moves quickly to the window.*)

FRIKKIE: (*At the window.*) I can see a cloud of dust.

SUSSIE: Maybe it's oom Piet. Bringing us something.

FRIKKIE: No. He only comes once a month. I think I know who it is. I've been expecting him.

SUSSIE: Who is he?

FRIKKIE: Oom Piet brought me a letter from him. Tant Riekie asked him to come and…see how we are. Now he's turning in at the gate. He must have cut the chain.

ALINA: You must drink your coffee Basie.

FRIKKIE: I don't want anything.

ALINA: (*Imperiously.*) You must drink it!

(*FRIKKIE drinks his coffee.*)

I know him. I know he's coming today. (*Touches her eyelids.*) I see.

SUSSIE: What do you see, old Alina?

ALINA: I know many fings. Many, maaany fings. But I not say.

(*ALINA exits to the kitchen. FRIKKIE back at the window.*)

SUSSIE: Is he coming to visit Ma and Pa? Is he?

FRIKKIE: Ma and Pa aren't here! Today you must open your eyes and see what's out there! The mangy cow, the two thin chickens…the rusted plough…and the broken tractor with its wheels in the sand!

SUSSIE: You're not nice to me.

FRIKKIE: I'm sorry.

SUSSIE: Why aren't you nice to me?

FRIKKIE: It's because the man is coming. (*Looks through window.*) He'll be here in a few minutes…and he'll want to know everything…how many cows…where are the crops…everything…and we'll have to tell him. But don't be afraid, Sussie… Don't be afraid.

---

2 Literally: 'little boss'. Used when a black adult of either sex addresses a white boy or a young white male. The term is used to convey respect and affection.

3 Used when a black adult of either sex addresses a white girl or a young white woman. The term is used to convey respect and affection.

SUSSIE: (*Suddenly excited.*) He's a visitor. We must give him tea. A visitor always gets tea. I'll call old Alina and tell her to take out the good cup and the white serviettes and the small silver teaspoons. (*Mother's voice.*) But you must get dressed, Frederik. Just look at you! When visitors are expected, you must dress neatly, do you hear me? Are your nails clean? Have you washed behind your ears? Do your shoes shine? Now go and put on your white shirt and your long pants and then you stay inside until the people come, or otherwise you'll mess up your clean clothes again.

FRIKKIE: (*Sulking.*) I don't have a white shirt, and my long pants are too small...

SUSSIE: (*Excited. Own voice.*) I know!

FRIKKIE: What?

(*SUSSIE runs to the chest.*)

SUSSIE: Ja! Ja...in here...look! (*Opens chest.*)

FRIKKIE: (*Running forward and banging the lid closed.*) Don't do that! Never open that!

SUSSIE: But what must I wear...? My clothes are all old and torn...I'm ashamed...I'm ashamed... What will the man say?

FRIKKIE: If you open that...something terrible will happen.

SUSSIE: Let's just open it...and see. Please. Just a little bit and then we'll see.

FRIKKIE: Just don't blame me, that's all.

(*SUSSIE opens the lid cautiously.*)

SUSSIE: See! Just old clothes. Nothing to be frightened of.

(*Starts rummaging through the old clothes.*)

FRIKKIE: (*Approaches and then turns away.*) I can smell them!

SUSSIE: It's not so bad.

FRIKKIE: It's getting stronger! The whole room...stinks of them.

(*FRIKKIE opens the window and leans out.*)

FRIKKIE: He's stopped again. What's he doing?

SUSSIE: (*Takes out a man's jacket.*) Look! A nice jacket! (*Rummages again.*) And trousers! You must put them on.

FRIKKIE: I won't touch them! Put them away.

SUSSIE: (*Mother's voice.*) And what are you going to wear? Just look at you!

FRIKKIE: I don't care!

SUSSIE: (*Mother's voice.*) You should be ashamed.

FRIKKIE: Just leave me alone!

SUSSIE: (*Own voice.*) Suit yourself! (*Continues to rummage.*)

FRIKKIE: (*At the window.*) It won't be long now…

SUSSIE: Boetie… I'll look nice in this dress… Do you remember? Ma used to wear it to church on Sundays… and also to funerals. And look! Here are shoes for me too! And here is Ma's fox! See how its eyes shine! And gloves…one glove! (*Mother's voice.*) I'm ready, my husband. Frederik! Susarah! Come at once, or we'll be late for the funeral.

(*FRIKKIE goes to the chest and slams down the lid.*)

Aren't you glad we have a guest?

FRIKKIE: He's not a guest.

SUSSIE: At least I know how to entertain a guest. (*Preens. Smoothes down her dress.*) It almost feels like Sunday after church. Remember, Boetie? (*Mother's voice.*) Come now, children…you can have a piece of cake and a little tart… and then you must go outside. But don't make a noise, and don't play because, remember, it's the Sabbath day. Susarah come back here! Go and take off your church hat! (*Own voice.*) And the aunties…when they bent down to kiss me…their pearls…touched my cheek…

FRIKKIE: (*At window.*) He's at the main gate…

SUSSIE: And the uncles!

FRIKKIE: He's stopped. What's he doing? He's taking pictures! Why is he taking pictures?

SUSSIE: They just lifted me up when they wanted to kiss me…

FRIKKIE: (*Jumps away from the window.*) He nearly saw me. He's taking a picture of the house.

SUSSIE: Doll… Big Girl…what a big girl you are…

FRIKKIE: He's getting into his car again.

SUSSIE: Do you remember…we always sat on the front steps and listened to the grown-ups in the dining room…the cups and the teaspoons sounded like little bells…?

FRIKKIE: He's near the shed.

SUSSIE: The starched tablecloth…and all the shining silver things…

(*ALINA appears in the kitchen door. She looks at them and then lays her finger across her lips. They listen silently as the car approaches and then stops. Car door opens and shuts. Gate creaks. Footsteps. GROVÉ knocks. Knocks again. FRIKKIE moves swiftly to the door and opens it. ALINA watches motionlessly.*)

GROVÉ: (*Enters. He is carrying a briefcase.*) Mr Cilliers? Miss Cilliers? Let me introduce myself. I'm Mr Grové – from Bloemfontein –

SUSSIE: Mr Grové, Mr Grové. What a nice name!

GROVÉ: I'm representing Miss Hendrica Cilliers, also from Bloemfontein.

SUSSIE: It's Aunt Riekie. How is Aunt Riekie? When she visited us, she brought five suitcases – one just for shoes. She always slept in the copper bed in the spare room...but now Piet van Rensburg's taken that away too... (*Mother's voice.*) Please come in, Mr Grové.

GROVÉ: (*Looking around in consternation.*) If you forgive me saying... This is all quite a shock. I never expected... anything like this. Let me be quite honest. I've never seen white people living like this.

FRIKKIE: You can leave if you want to.

GROVÉ: I'm here on business, miss. (*Rubs his forehead.*) How could I have imagined? I mean...not in my wildest dreams. (*Clears his throat.*) I'm sorry to have to tell you, but your aunt passed away quite suddenly. (*Takes an envelope out of his breast-pocket.*) Your aunt wrote you a letter shortly before her death.

FRIKKIE: Thank you. (*Taking it.*)

SUSSIE: I want it! Give it to me!

GROVÉ: Please! I think it would be better if I read it to you. I don't want to be the cause of any disagreement.
(*FRIKKIE gives the letter to GROVÉ.*)
(*Opening the letter. Muttering as if to himself.*) It's so late. I should have got here earlier...but everyone gave me different directions.
(*ALINA returns to the kitchen.*)
(*Reads very drily.*) 'My dear niece and nephew, I wish I could see you but as you know I'm bedridden. My poor heart doesn't seem to beat. It only flutters weakly. I'm covered in bedsores. My skin has become so thin. I'm all

alone now. I only have half-blind old Mietie who sleeps on a mat next to my bed. I know the end is near and I have left all my worldly possessions to you. Mr Grové will know what to do. Your long-suffering aunt Riekie.'

SUSSIE: (*Own voice.*) Thank you. That was a nice letter. I'm sorry Aunt Riekie's dead. I'm very sorry. (*Mother's voice.*) Please won't you make yourself at home. Wouldn't you like a nice refreshing cup of tea?

GROVÉ: (*Confused.*) Thank you, miss...but I really don't think so. I can't stay for very long. I...don't want to drive on these dirt-roads in the dark.

SUSSIE: (*Mother's voice, very loud.*) Alina! Bring the tea! And remember...the good cup! Please sit down, Mr Grové. I'm sorry I can't offer you anything to eat...I would have baked today, but the hens are laying so badly at the moment. They are distressed because the cock died recently.

FRIKKIE: What can we do for you?

GROVÉ: Well...I had some business matters to discuss with you. But now...things have changed. You see...I didn't quite expect this. Your aunt was deeply concerned about you... But she could hardly have imagined... Mr Cilliers, I think there are some questions I need to ask you, if you don't mind, as the executor of your aunt's will.

FRIKKIE: What do you want to ask?

SUSSIE: (*Mother's voice, very loudly. GROVÉ starts.*) And Alina did you remember the small teaspoons? (*Mutters.*) I've told her a thousand times, but with these people...

ALINA: (*From the kitchen.*) Ja, Nonnie.

GROVÉ: Well, let me begin then. (*GROVÉ waves flies away from his face.*) You should do something about these flies... Firstly I want particulars...concerning your last crop. (*ALINA enters with tea things on a tray. She arranges them on the table.*)

SUSSIE: (*Mother's voice.*) Thank you Alina. That'll be all.

FRIKKIE: I can give you no...'particulars'...concerning crops. (*ALINA exits to the kitchen.*)

SUSSIE: (*Mother's voice.*) Milk, Mr Grové?

GROVÉ: Please, miss. What are you implying?

SUSSIE: (*Mother's voice.*) Sugar, Mr Grové?

GROVÉ: Please, miss.

SUSSIE: (*Mother's voice.*) How many, Mr Grové?

GROVÉ: One please, miss. Aren't you having tea?

SUSSIE: (*Own voice.*) No, we just drank our coffee. We always drink coffee when we wake up.

GROVÉ: You mean…you've just woken up?

SUSSIE: Yes.

GROVÉ: But…the sun is going down.

FRIKKIE: That's right.

GROVÉ: I…see…

FRIKKIE: You know that there haven't been any crops. I saw you looking around out there. And what did you see, meneer? Weeds? No, not even that, because nothing grows in the dust. What did you expect? Tell me. Rippling cornfields? Sunflowers? Mealies? No! That you won't find here! Only acres and acres – as far as the eye can see – of bone dry, scorched earth.

SUSSIE: (*Mother's voice.*) Your tea, Mr Grové!

GROVÉ: Thank you. (*Takes the cup.*) Well then Mr Cilliers, I'll have to write – 'no crop'.

FRIKKIE: Write what you like.

GROVÉ: And would you ascribe the lack of productivity to the severe drought?

FRIKKIE: You can say it's the drought.

SUSSIE: When Frikkie and I were small, it rained a lot. Yes it did! In the evening I used to lie in bed and…listen to the rain on the roof. I like sleeping when it rains.

GROVÉ: And when the drought is broken, do you think you could make a fresh start?

SUSSIE: Near my window the rain dripped from the long roof onto the verandah roof. And between the drip… drip… I could hear the dahlias…growing.

FRIKKIE: The rain won't come.

SUSSIE: Yes, the dahlias grew all night – and all the new buds opened slowly. There were pink ones, red ones and yellow ones…

GROVÉ: How can you be sure, Mr Cilliers?

SUSSIE: But the white ones were the biggest. In the dark they shone…like stars.

FRIKKIE: I know. I know that it won't rain again.

GROVÉ: If you don't mind me saying so…that's a ridiculous statement. There are only a few more questions I want to ask you. It's getting very dark. Could we have some light, please miss. (*Puts down the cup.*)

SUSSIE: (*Mother's voice.*) Alina! Have you lit the lamps?

ALINA: Ja, Nonnie.

GROVÉ: It's getting late…

SUSSIE: (*Mother's voice.*) Well, why don't you bring them, Alina? At once!

GROVÉ: I wanted to come sooner, but there were so many things to attend to at the office.

(*ALINA enters.*)

SUSSIE: (*Mother's voice.*) Put that one on the table, Alina, and that one next to the bed. And Alina, take the tray with you…and don't forget the candle for the washroom!

GROVÉ: Tell me, Mr Cilliers, are the fences in good repair?

FRIKKIE: As you've seen, blown over and trampled down.

SUSSIE: (*Own voice.*) And when it was very hot…they used to wilt…

GROVÉ: Would I be correct in saying, Mr Cilliers, that you have not contributed to the upkeep of this farm?

SUSSIE: Ma cut out all the dead flowers every day…

FRIKKIE: I work too hard. I don't have time for fences. You talk about fences! And the river dried up long ago!

SUSSIE: He really works hard. Very hard. Wait…wait… don't move! (*Swats fly on GROVÉ.*) It's dead! Flies are dirty things. My mother says… they bring germs into the house. And do you know what? They lay their eggs in dung. Yes! In dung! That's where they hatch out…

FRIKKIE: Be quiet, Sussie!

SUSSIE: And then they come and sit on our food.

FRIKKIE: Stop it! The man wants to know about fences. Well, why don't you write. Write! 'The wire fences are in disrepair and the gates – where there still are gates – are sagging on their rusted hinges. No repairs have been made since the sudden death of Pieter Frederik Cilliers, the previous owner of the farm.'

(*SUSSIE twirls the fly-swatter around her finger. It makes a whirring noise.*)

GROVÉ: And when was that? When were your parents...
When did the tragedy occur?

FRIKKIE: I don't know.

GROVÉ: I only want the year.

(*ALINA enters with a slops bucket.*)

FRIKKIE: I don't know. Sometimes it feels like long ago and
other times...like yesterday.

GROVÉ: Miss, can you tell me in which year your parents
were...how shall I say...

(*ALINA kneels next to the bed.*)

SUSSIE: I don't know. The one day they were alive and the
next they were dead.

FRIKKIE: It was just before the drought. Now when was that?
When was the last time it rained? When did I last hear
thunder...see lightning?

(*ALINA empties the chamber-pot into the slops bucket.*)

GROVÉ: Never mind...never mind. I'll get the particulars
myself. I'll look it up when I get back. No one will forget
that in a hurry. Not the robbery and murder. That happens
every day. But mutilation!

(*ALINA exits with the slops bucket. Silence as GROVÉ watches
her.*)

(*Confiding. Low voice.*) To do something like that! It's
because they hate us, and that's the truth! They'd like to
kill and torture every one of us! You can see it in their eyes!

(*SUSSIE starts crying.*)

FRIKKIE: You've upset my sister! Why couldn't you keep
your big mouth shut!

(*ALINA enters, and as GROVÉ continues to speak, she goes to
SUSSIE, puts her arms around her and gently rocks her.*)

GROVÉ: I'm sorry. I didn't mean to upset her. After all, she
knows about it, doesn't she? And it's not like it happened
yesterday.

FRIKKIE: (*Shouting.*) We don't want to think about it!! Do you
hear me! Do you know what it's like? Opening a door...
and finding that? Do you know!!

GROVÉ: I'm...very sorry.

FRIKKIE: Have you ever seen an arm without a hand! Have
you ever...

31

GROVÉ: (*Almost tearful.*) Please! I'm extremely sorry. I wasn't thinking. I won't mention another word. I suppose I can understand…

FRIKKIE: (*Coldly.*) You understand nothing.

GROVÉ: What I mean is… I mean…it must have been a terrible shock. I mean…it certainly could explain…your circumstances. Let me say again that I'm very sorry.

FRIKKIE: Don't apologise to me. It's my sister who's unhappy.

GROVÉ: Of course…of course… (*Gets up and approaches SUSSIE tentatively.*)

ALINA: (*Lifts her head and glares at him. Speaks with extreme violence.*) Au Sooka![4]

GROVÉ: What did you say to me? Watch yourself! (*To FRIKKIE.*) She looks…dangerous to me. I wouldn't trust her if I were you. Statistics show that there is very often an insider involved in these brutal murders. They're the ones who supply the information. Who open the doors while everyone is asleep.

FRIKKIE: She won't stop. Sometimes she cries for days. It nearly drives me mad!

GROVÉ: But can't you tell her that I'm sorry.

FRIKKIE: That won't help. (*Short silence.*) There is…one thing.

GROVÉ: What?

FRIKKIE: If you can…give her a present.

GROVÉ: But I don't have anything.

FRIKKIE: I know what she likes. (*Opens GROVÉ's briefcase.*)

GROVÉ: Leave that alone! Those are important papers!
(*FRIKKIE turns the briefcase upside down. The papers fall out.*)
Now see what you've done!

FRIKKIE: I heard something falling.

GROVÉ: (*Kneeling and picking up papers.*) That's just my toothbrush and my toothpaste. When I'm away from home all day, I always take them with me. I brush my teeth after each meal.

FRIKKIE: (*Picks up a small box.*) This?

GROVÉ: Pills…for indigestion.

4 A Sotho phrase meaning 'To hell with you!'

FRIKKIE: (*Picks up a tube of ointment.*) And this?

GROVÉ: Ointment. For my eczema. Please just leave my things alone! (*He gets up and puts the papers back in the briefcase.*)

FRIKKIE: What's in there? In your pocket?

GROVÉ: It's my wallet. Only identity documents and money.

FRIKKIE: Let me see.

GROVÉ: You have no right.

FRIKKIE: (*Menacingly.*) Give it to me!
(*GROVÉ reluctantly hands over the wallet to FRIKKIE. FRIKKIE looks through the wallet.*)
What are these?

GROVÉ: They're photographs of my family.

FRIKKIE: Nice. Sussie likes pictures.

GROVÉ: But they belong to me!

FRIKKIE: Go over there and give them to her.

GROVÉ: I'll do no such thing.

FRIKKIE: (*With quiet menace.*) If she doesn't stop crying soon, I don't know what I'll do.

GROVÉ: All right then. (*Mutters.*) At least I have the negatives. (*Approaches SUSSIE cautiously.*) Miss…

FRIKKIE: Don't call her that. Call her 'my little doll'.

GROVÉ: I'm really very sorry, but…

FRIKKIE: Otherwise you might as well forget it!

GROVÉ: Very well then. (*Holds the pictures out to her.*) My… My…

FRIKKIE: (*Prompting.*) Little doll.

GROVÉ: Little doll.
(*SUSSIE looks up. She stops crying. She takes the photographs and looks at them. She seems pleased.*
ALINA looks at GROVÉ, then she gets up and goes back to the kitchen.)
Well… I'm glad everything has been…amicably resolved.
(*He mops his brow with his handkerchief.*)
(*Short silence.*)
Cilliers, if you don't mind…there is just one more question I must ask you.

FRIKKIE: That will have to wait… I'll be back just now…but it's getting late and I must go and put the cow in the shed. You can talk to Sussie.

GROVÉ: No. Wait!
  (*FRIKKIE exits, whistling.*
  Silence while whistling gets softer and softer as FRIKKIE moves
  further away.)
SUSSIE: (*After a silence.*) Why are you so quiet? (*Giggles.*)
  You know what they say: 'Still water, deep ground, and
  underneath the Devil is turning round.'
GROVÉ: (*Clears throat.*) I really hope your brother will be
  back soon, because I should be going. My wife gets very
  worried when I'm late.
SUSSIE: These are nice pictures.
GROVÉ: Thank you, miss.
SUSSIE: Did you take these pictures?
GROVÉ: Well, yes. (*Shy laugh.*) I'm a bit of an…amateur
  photographer. It's my hobby.
SUSSIE: (*Looking at the photographs.*) Who's that?
GROVÉ: That's my wife. Mrs Grové.
SUSSIE: Oe, but she's pretty.
GROVÉ: Thank you, miss.
SUSSIE: She's got red nails and a red mouth. Is she bad?
GROVÉ: Certainly not.
SUSSIE: My mother says that women who want to improve
  on God's work are wicked and damned.
GROVÉ: I can assure you that my wife…
SUSSIE: (*Looking at another photograph.*) And who's this?
GROVÉ: It's our firstborn, Johan. He's been named after
  my father – Johannes Gerhardus Jacobus. Yes, he's his
  grandfather and grandmother's pride and joy.
SUSSIE: He's sweet.
GROVÉ: And bright! He's only three, but his favourite word
  is: 'whatsat?' Yes, he wants to know everything. And he's
  very fond of me. You mustn't think that he'll go to sleep
  before I get home. He'll be wide awake, because he's
  waiting for his 'dadda'. (*Silence.*) It…becomes cold here in
  the evenings. You can almost say that this part of the world
  is getting a desert climate; hot in the day and cold…at
  night. (*Clears throat.*) I hope your brother gets back soon.
  It's getting very late.
SUSSIE: (*Looking at another photograph.*) And there *you* are!

GROVÉ: (*Looking over her shoulder.*) Yes. That was taken on our honeymoon in Durban.

SUSSIE: You're sitting so close together.

GROVÉ: (*Embarrassed.*) Yes…

SUSSIE: Are you sitting in a wagon?

GROVÉ: No. It's a rickshaw.

SUSSIE: What's that?

GROVÉ: A…small cart drawn by a single person.

SUSSIE: That black man with the feathers and the leopard skin? Is that him?

GROVÉ: Yes.

SUSSIE: Just look at the pretty wagon with all the colours. Both of you are smiling.

GROVÉ: I remember, it was a nice day. Very still. And the sea was calm.
(*Short silence. In the distance, the lowing of a cow can be heard.*)

SUSSIE: You're so lucky. I've never seen the sea.

GROVÉ: One day you will, miss.

SUSSIE: One day… But just look at me. I'm not like her. I'm not pretty.

GROVÉ: That's not true.

SUSSIE: (*Tearful.*) I don't look like her. Powdered face and blood red nails. (*Whispers.*) Those things are of the devil. Broad is the road to damnation. (*Aloud.*) I don't have a nice dress like her. And pretty shoes. (*Pause.*) No one will want to sit close to me.

GROVÉ: That's not true, miss.

SUSSIE: Really? Will you? Will you sit next to me like that?

GROVÉ: I really don't think…

SUSSIE: I knew you wouldn't. (*Tearful.*) I told you so. I put on this dress for you. I put on…these shoes. (*Now very upset.*) But you won't sit next to me! Is it…because I'm dirty? Is it? Tell me!

GROVÉ: (*Nervously.*) Don't upset yourself miss. What will your brother say? (*Short silence.*) If you wish, then… But only for a moment.

SUSSIE: Thank you. Thank you! I have some of my Ma's *eau de Cologne*. I'll put it on for you. (*Finds the cologne on the bedside table.*) Where must I put it? (*Opens the bottle.*) Here!

(*Throws her head back.*) Here… (*She puts a drop in the hollow of her neck.*) Now I smell nice. (*Sits on the side of the bed.*) Now you must come and sit.

(*GROVÉ reluctantly sits down next to her.*)

Just like you sat with her. You must put your arm around my shoulder.

(*GROVÉ reluctantly puts his arm around her shoulder.*)

You must put your cheek next to mine.

(*GROVÉ put his cheek next to hers. He looks acutely uncomfortable.*)

You must hold my hand.

(*GROVÉ holds her hand.*)

And now we must smile and smile.

(*SUSSIE smiles but GROVÉ does not.*)

(*Speaking while she still looks out front and smiles blandly.*)

Oe, your hand is so soft. Not like Frikkie's hand. He has callouses and his skin is rough. But yours…

GROVÉ: (*Drawing away.*) I think that's enough.

SUSSIE: (*Pulling him close to her. Speaks breathlessly and seductively.*) Mine are also rough and ugly. It's because of all the work. But my skin is soft in other places…

Very soft. (*She guides his hand under her skirt.*)

(*GROVÉ seems too fascinated to resist. FRIKKIE appears in the door and watches.*)

(*Continuing to guide GROVÉ's hand.*) Soft…and white… and smooth. It's so…nice… Your soft skin…touching… (*Her head drops onto his shoulder.*)

(*FRIKKIE makes a sound. GROVÉ jumps up.*)

GROVÉ: I'm sorry…terribly sorry…but…it's *her*.

SUSSIE: (*Speaking very fast.*) What'll Ma say? Ma will be angry… Ma will say I'm bad… A bad girl… A disgrace to our family…

GROVÉ: It's not what you think…

FRIKKIE: Stop it, Sussie! You must forget about those things. (*Pause. To GROVÉ.*) You wanted to ask me a question. What was it?

GROVÉ: (*Distracted, trying to collect his thoughts.*) Yes… I wanted to know… By the way, why is there a hole in your floor? Are you removing termites?

(*SUSSIE sits on the bed. She starts systematically tearing up the photographs.*)

FRIKKIE: Maybe.

GROVÉ: I was just asking. (*Noticing what SUSSIE is doing.*) Look at what she's doing! Can't you stop her? Please!

FRIKKIE: You stop her if you want to.

(*GROVÉ looks on in helpless dismay.*)

So…what is it that you wanted to know?

(*GROVÉ and SUSSIE together.*)

GROVÉ: I wanted to know how you can afford to stay on here, if you're not producing any crops. Or do you have any alternative source of income?

SUSSIE: (*Sing-song as if to herself.*) You're a bad girl! Wicked! Wicked! A bad, bad girl! You bad…bad…bad girl! (*Scatters the fragments of photographs.*)

FRIKKIE: Stop it, Sussie! (*Stretches out on the bed next to her.*) Now let me see…

(*Silence, while GROVÉ waits with pen poised.*)

Every month Piet van Rensburg comes with his lorry and brings us everything we need: paraffin, salt, soap, toilet-paper… And then he takes what he wants.

SUSSIE: (*Excited.*) Ma's harmonium – she used to play hymns and psalms on it – the four-poster, the stinkwood table…

FRIKKIE: And so, you see…each month I sell our birthright for table salt and toilet paper.

SUSSIE: The…the wardrobe…the washstand…and now all the rooms are empty – Ma's and Pa's and mine and Boetie's – and so Boetie nailed up the doors, didn't you, Boetie?

GROVÉ: Really, Mr Cilliers, your aunt would have been very unhappy about all this. If she'd known…

FRIKKIE: For the portrait of our great uncle, the Boergeneral, we got two chickens and the tripe of six sheep.

SUSSIE: And a ribbon for my hair. This one!

GROVÉ: This is shameful.

SUSSIE: We were glad when oom Piet took him away. His eyes were always looking at us.

FRIKKIE: Then there's the vegetable garden. Old Alina looks
after the vegetables…
SUSSIE: And I help Old Alina.
(*SUSSIE and FRIKKIE speak simultaneously.*)

FRIKKIE: Potatoes…	SUSSIE: Radishes…
carrots…pumpkin…	beans…
Beetroot…cabbages…	And peas…
There are also fruit trees.	Mulberries…

SUSSIE: But only Boetie picks them. It's too far away for me.
I can't go out of the front door. I can go out of the back
door. (*Fearful.*) But…I can't go out of the gate.
GROVÉ: And why not?
SUSSIE: (*Loud whisper.*) I'm not allowed to.
GROVÉ: Who said you weren't? Is it the black woman?
SUSSIE: No, it's not. It's…them.
GROVÉ: Who?
SUSSIE: Them! (*Fast and fearful.*) There are many places I
can't go… Many things I mustn't say. (*Claps her hand over
her mouth.*)
GROVÉ: But who…tells you not to do these things?
SUSSIE: They don't…tell me. I know. I know what they want.
FRIKKIE: Stop it, Sussie! I'm warning you!
GROVÉ: Who are these people she's talking about? I…don't
like what's going on here. There's something wrong and
that's a fact.
(*Short silence.*)
Just one or two more questions…and then I must be going.
(*He takes off his glasses, cleans them with his handkerchief and
puts them on again. Picks up a pen.*) Tell me Mr Cilliers…
during this time of drought, where do you get the water for
vegetables and fruit trees?
SUSSIE: Have you ever heard of underground water? (*Points
to FRIKKIE.*) And he found it! Frikkie found it. Come on
Boetie, tell him Boetie…
FRIKKIE: Stop it!
SUSSIE: Frikkie said he could hear water. Every night when
he put his head down on the pillow, he could hear water
running. Pa said he was dreaming and Ma said he had
wax in his ears, but he still heard it. Then old Alina said

it was under the ground. There are people who can hear things like that, she said. Then Pa started to believe him, and when the borehole people came, they looked for water near Frikkie's room and they just started to bore when the strong water came out. You should have seen it! And from that time, the windmill turns when the wind blows and the water comes out and it...

FRIKKIE: Stop it, Sussie! The man doesn't want to listen to your long stories. (*To GROVÉ.*) So you see, we can get along in our way...

SUSSIE: That's how it all started...and now our work is almost finished. (*She goes to the hole, picks up a tin and starts digging. She strews the earth out over the floor.*)

GROVÉ: (*Wiping earth from his shoe.*) But you can't be serious. You must realise that this can't continue. When you've traded all the furniture, what will happen then? How can you live here in a derelict house without any furniture, while this farm goes to rack and ruin? It's shameful that you just lie there and make no effort to improve the situation. I mean – a boer always makes a plan!

SUSSIE: (*Scared.*) Is he angry with us?

GROVÉ: I'm sorry. I shouldn't be speaking like this. I realise that you and your sister are not...responsible for your actions.

FRIKKIE: What do you mean by that?

GROVÉ: (*Closing case and getting up.*) I need to finalise the will. The sooner some decision is reached, the better.

FRIKKIE: What do you want to do? Are you afraid to tell us what you think of us? Are you afraid we'll get...angry?

GROVÉ: Not at all, Mr Cilliers. It is customary procedure, that is all. Well, I must be on my way. I have a long drive ahead of me. Goodbye, Mr Cilliers.
(*He extends his hand. FRIKKIE ignores him.*)
Goodbye miss. Thank you for the tea.
(*She ignores him. As he gets to the door she hits him on the back with a large clod of earth. Slowly turning around, very angry.*)
Maybe I can make an exception in your case. If you want my honest opinion, I'll give it to you. You're raving mad! Both of you! *Non compus mentis*!

SUSSIE: Is he swearing at us?

GROVÉ: But not too mad to know what you're doing. From the first moment, you've tried to confuse me, to… undermine me with your insanity! Since I arrived here, it's been one long nightmare! This is a madhouse!

SUSSIE: Please…don't be angry with us…please!

GROVÉ: You'll be hearing from me! It's going to be a pleasure to attend to this matter! (*Exits.*)

(*Footsteps fade away. Gate creaks open. Tries to start car. Tries again. FRIKKIE listens.*)

SUSSIE: His car's broken! But then he can't go away. I want him to go away!

FRIKKIE: Ssht. (*He listens tensely.*)

(*Another attempt but the car won't start. FRIKKIE thrusts his hands deep into his pockets and whistles tunelessly.*)

GROVÉ: (*Knocks. No response. Opens door and peers in.*) There's…something wrong with my car. Have you got a telephone? I don't know what to do. Do you know something about cars, Mr Cilliers?

(*ALINA appears in the kitchen doorway and watches him.*)

FRIKKIE: No. On the paraffin tin. The telephone.

SUSSIE: But Boetie…

FRIKKIE: Sshht.

GROVÉ: (*Turns handle.*) Hullo! Exchange! Exchange! Can you hear me? (*Turns handle again.*) Hullo exchange, can you hear me? (*To FRIKKIE.*) Why didn't you tell me that it's out of order? I suppose you think it's funny? (*Mutters.*) I should have expected it.

(*ALINA goes back to the kitchen. Short silence.*)

(*More friendly.*) How far is it to the neighbouring farm, Mr Cilliers?

FRIKKIE: About three miles. Or maybe…a little further…

GROVÉ: Three miles! That far?

SUSSIE: Ja.

GROVÉ: This is such a desolate part of the world. So… where is the farm? How do I get there? I suppose I have no choice. I can't stay here.

FRIKKIE: You see…it's like this. (*Indicates with straight arm.*) Down the steps… Through the gate…

GROVÉ: Yes… Yes. (*Takes out a pen and pocketbook.*)

FRIKKIE: Straight ahead. When you get to the cowshed you turn left and you walk and walk until you see the bluegums.

GROVÉ: (*Muttering as he writes.*) Bluegums…

SUSSIE: Ja. Ten bluegums. All in a ring.

FRIKKIE: (*Ominously as he moves closer to GROVÉ.*) But one thing… If you hear something close to you…

GROVÉ: What do you mean?

FRIKKIE: Something moving near you…
(*SUSSIE also moves closer to GROVÉ.*)
Or breathing…
(*SUSSIE makes ominous breathing noises.*)
Or panting…
(*SUSSIE hangs her tongue out and makes panting noises.*)
Then you just keep walking. Never stop. Never look around. And never run. (*Losing interest and moving away.*) Then you go right.

GROVÉ: At…the bluegums?

FRIKKIE: Ja. Sharp right. Past the dam.

SUSSIE: (*Looking over GROVÉ's shoulder.*) It used to be a dam but now it's only a big hole in the ground.

FRIKKIE: And then you'll find the road. If you look veeery carefully you'll see it's a road. And you go left until you see 'Môreson'[5] on a disc – you know, a plow-disc. It's very faded now but that's the place.

GROVÉ: (*Reading rapidly.*) Left at cowshed, right at bluegums, left into road.

SUSSIE: See? It's easy!

GROVÉ: You say it's about three miles?

FRIKKIE: Ja.

SUSSIE: Ja.

GROVÉ: And there's nothing closer?

FRIKKIE: No.

SUSSIE: No. (*Excited.*) Why don't you stay over? We have a pillow…and an eiderdown!

GROVÉ: Thank you, miss, but I'm in a hurry. Are you sure you don't know anything about cars, Mr Cilliers?

5 Morning Sun

FRIKKIE: Yes. I mean no, I don't.

SUSSIE: No.

GROVÉ: Well, I'd better be going. You…don't have a torch?

FRIKKIE: A torch?

GROVÉ: Yes. You see…it's very dark out there. There's no moon tonight.

FRIKKIE: No.

GROVÉ: Well then…goodbye Mr Cilliers. Goodbye miss. I'll bring someone back to help me with the car but I won't… bother you again.

SUSSIE: Are you sure you can't stay over? We don't get many guests.

GROVÉ: I'm sure… Well, goodbye.

(GROVÉ exits. Sound of car door opening. GROVÉ tries to start the car. He tries again and again until the battery starts running down. While this is happening FRIKKIE whistles softly. Then he takes the alternator out of his back pocket and drops it down the excavation.)

SUSSIE: I…don't think he likes us, Boetie. *(Silence.)* He's different. I don't know how different. Maybe he's shorter – or maybe he only looks shorter because he's so pale. What do you think, Boetie?

FRIKKIE: Maybe.

(Car door being slammed. Footsteps receding.)

SUSSIE: And he has more hair than Pa. What do you think?

FRIKKIE: *(Sullen.)* Ja…that's right. *(Short silence.)* But not much more.

(Short silence.)

SUSSIE: Boetie, are you angry with me?

FRIKKIE: No.

SUSSIE: Have I done something wrong again?

FRIKKIE: I tell you. It's just that…I'm scared things will go wrong.

SUSSIE: What do you mean?

FRIKKIE: I don't know.

SUSSIE: You're scaring me.

FRIKKIE: It'll be all right. You'll see.

SUSSIE: Do you think so?

FRIKKIE: Ja…I think so.

(*Silence. SUSSIE watches FRIKKIE.*)

SUSSIE: Come on Boetie. We haven't played today. It'll be so nice.

FRIKKIE: You'll see… He'll get lost and turn back.

SUSSIE: Then we'll stop. Come on. And we can play just what you want to play. Then we won't be scared any more.

FRIKKIE: All right then…

SUSSIE: What do you want to play?

FRIKKIE: I don't know.

SUSSIE: 'Listening at Ma and Pa's bedroom door'?

FRIKKIE: Not really…we played it yesterday.

SUSSIE: Do you want to play 'Pa is angry with Sussie'?

FRIKKIE: No…not that. We always have to play that.

SUSSIE: What about 'Ma asks Frederik about the sheets'?

FRIKKIE: Yes, that's a nice one. But it's too long.

SUSSIE: We can stop when we want to. Please Boetie. Can we play it, Boetie?

FRIKKIE: Ja.

SUSSIE: Let's get ready then!

(*SUSSIE pins up her hair and FRIKKIE gets the soap-box and places it carefully in the centre of the stage.*)

Are you ready, Frikkie?

FRIKKIE: Ja. I am.

SUSSIE: (*Who assumes a stern voice and a grown-up persona for the rest of the game.*) Frederik!

FRIKKIE: (*Bashful little boy.*) Ja Ma?

SUSSIE: (*Speaks to imaginary person.*) No Sussie, my child, you can't come with us. You haven't finished your darning. Come on, Frederik. My goodness, but the sun is hot today! Frederick go and put on your khaki hat. (*To imaginary ALINA.*) Alina! Remember to take out the rusks when they're ready…and keep the flies off them when they come out!

(*FRIKKIE puts on the khaki hat.*)

Come now.

(*They walk in a wide circle, SUSSIE in front and FRIKKIE trailing behind.*)

The dahlias are looking good… Oh no! Do you see the weeds? I'll have to talk to Jonas!

(*They walk to front centre-stage.*) Open the gate, my child.
(*FRIKKIE opens imaginary gate.*)
And close the gate. Do you want the chickens to get out?
(*Closes gate. Pause. SUSSIE clears her throat.*)
Well Boet…now that we're alone, there's something I want
to talk to you about.

FRIKKIE: What is it Ma? Have I done something wrong Ma?

SUSSIE: (*Feeding chickens.*) Kie-ie-iep kiep kiep kiep kiep.
Kie-ie-iep kiep kiep. Well…you see, my son…it's just
that…you've messed again.

FRIKKIE: …Messed, Ma?

SUSSIE: Ja, my child. Kie-ie-iep kiep kiep kiep kiep. You…
messed all over your sheets again. You know I look at
your sheets every morning. Look at me when I talk to you
Frederik!

FRIKKIE: I'm sorry, Ma.

SUSSIE: My child…you see, I want to help you… These
things my son, these things are of the devil. There's an egg,
my child. (*Points.*) There!
(*FRIKKIE bends down and picks up imaginary egg.*)
Put it here in my basket. Thank you son. What was I
saying? Oh yes. Something like this only happens when
you have…dirty thoughts. And where do these thoughts
come from? From Satan, my child, from Satan.

FRIKKIE: Ja Ma…I know, Ma.

SUSSIE: That's good, my son. That's good. There's another
egg, son. There, under the little black hen.

FRIKKIE: Here, Ma.

SUSSIE: Thank you, son. A funny colour. As I was saying,
my son…these things are of the devil. Your father said he'd
thrash it out of you…this wickedness. But I asked him to
let me speak to you first, to see if you couldn't repent and
be saved. If you can only talk to me openly, my son. If you
can tell me about these…wicked… filthy…thoughts…then
you will be healed, because evil deeds and evil thoughts
breed in darkness and secrecy. Do you understand, my
son?

FRIKKIE: Ja Ma, I understand.

SUSSIE: There are two more. There! Under the straw. Thank you Frederik. And now...will you confess...will you tell me...everything?

FRIKKIE: Ja Ma. I will, Ma.

SUSSIE: Now come and sit here...in the shade of the... apricot tree.

FRIKKIE: Ja, Ma.

(*They sit on the upside-down soap-box.*)

SUSSIE: Now tell me, my son... Tell me... What do you think about...before you go to sleep at night?

FRIKKIE: I think about everything that happened on the farm that day, Ma.

SUSSIE: No, my son. You don't understand what I mean. I'm talking about...filthy thoughts. Do you have...filthy thoughts before you go to sleep my son?

FRIKKIE: Well, Ma...

SUSSIE: Come now Boet... Are you going to tell me or not?

FRIKKIE: Well Ma...sometimes I think about...girls...

SUSSIE: How do you think about...these girls? In what way?

FRIKKIE: I think how pretty they are...the girls that I've seen... Their hair so long and shining. And then I wonder what it would feel like to...touch their hair.

SUSSIE: And...what else, my son?

FRIKKIE: And I think...how soft girls are.

SUSSIE: Soft, my son?

FRIKKIE: Ja Ma. Soft...and round. Not like boys, Ma. Not so hard...and rough. But soft...

SUSSIE: Go on, my child.

FRIKKIE: And I think how nice it would be if I could touch their...warm...soft...round...

SUSSIE: Yes, my son? Yes?

FRIKKIE: (*Quickly and shyly.*) Their breasts, Ma. Their breasts.

SUSSIE: (*Clasps her hands together.*) Oh, my son. My poor son. You have been led into temptation.

FRIKKIE: Ja Ma. I know, Ma.

SUSSIE: And...tell me, my son...do you dream? Do you dream...about unholy things?

FRIKKIE: I don't know Ma.

SUSSIE: What did you dream last night… Last night when you…messed like that? Come now, my son. You must tell me everything… You must be delivered from evil.

FRIKKIE: Well Ma. Let me think, Ma. (*Gets up and walks about.*)

SUSSIE: Careful Frederik! You almost stepped on a hen! When you're in here, you must be careful.

FRIKKIE: Ja Ma. Sorry Ma.

SUSSIE: (*With veiled eagerness.*) You were going to tell me about your dream, my child. Come and sit here next to me. I'm waiting.

FRIKKIE: (*Sits and thinks.*) Ja… Ja…now I remember. I dreamt that I…woke up. It was late and everybody was asleep. I could see the moon through the window. A big, yellow full moon. Something woke me up. A sound. I lay still and listened but I couldn't hear anything… Only Pa snoring and the crickets. Then I heard it again… Something moving out there in the garden. I pushed up the window and jumped down into the dahlias. I started walking through the dahlias… They were very big and high above my head. And then I saw something… between the flowers…on the ground… Slowly…slowly I walked nearer… Shoe! I was scared Ma…very scared. And then I saw it was a woman!

SUSSIE: A woman, my son?

FRIKKIE: Ma. Lying there…half buried under the wet earth.

SUSSIE: Was she…fully clothed, my son?

FRIKKIE: No, Ma.

SUSSIE: Was she…naked, my son?

FRIKKIE: Ja, Ma.

SUSSIE: Oh, deliver us from evil! And…then my son?

FRIKKIE: I thought she was dead. I crouched down next to her… She opened her eyes…they shone in the dark…and then she said: 'I'm not dead. I'm not cold. Touch me.'

SUSSIE: And…did you, my son?

FRIKKIE: Ja. I put out my hand…and I touched her.

SUSSIE: Where, my son?

FRIKKIE: Ma?

SUSSIE: Where exactly did you touch her?

FRIKKIE: (*Gets up and walks about excitedly.*) Everywhere, Ma. Everywhere.

SUSSIE: Save and protect us!

FRIKKIE: (*Excited.*) And she was hot, Ma. Hot…as if a fire burned inside her. (*Look of disgust.*) Sies! (*Lifts up foot.*)

SUSSIE: Now why did you have to go and step in that, my son? Scrape it off on the low wall over there. I don't want you to get that on my floors. That's right. What happened then? Come and sit down. Now tell me.

FRIKKIE: And then a cold wind came up. I asked her if she didn't want to come into the house. I told her it was getting cold and that my Ma would give her clothes to put on and coffee to drink. But she just lay there and looked at me with her shining eyes. I told her that I would have to go in then, because I was very cold.

SUSSIE: That's good, my child.

FRIKKIE: But she said, 'Come and lie with me…I'll make you warm…I'll cover you with my hair.' And then I saw her hair, Ma…dark hair…everywhere…all around her… between the dahlias…and as far as I could see…

SUSSIE: And did you, my son? Did you lie with her?

FRIKKIE: I wanted Ma… I really wanted to… And so I did…with my head…

SUSSIE: Your head, my son?

FRIKKIE: Between her breasts Ma… Between her breasts.

SUSSIE: Oh, hell and damnation!

FRIKKIE: And she covered me with her hair…soft hair…she covered me with her hair until I couldn't see anything any more… Not the flowers or the moon… Nothing. Everything was dark and I lay close to her. She was soft and warm…and I could feel her heart beating… It was beating like a drum… Beating…beating…and then I woke up.

SUSSIE: My poor son. My poor child. Tell me Boetie…did you look closely at this woman? This…manifestation of evil? Could you see the devil's cunning in her face?

FRIKKIE: Ja Ma. I looked at her face Ma. I felt…as if I knew her, Ma. (*Excited.*) Hey! Ma! She looked like you, Ma!

SUSSIE: How dare you! How dare you! You're bad. That's
what you are! You're wicked! (*Rushes towards the 'house'.*)
Come, my husband. Come and drive the evil spirits out!
(*Pause. SUSSIE starts giggling. She turns around.*)
(*Own voice.*) And then Ma dropped the eggs and they all
broke! Do you remember Boetie?
(*No response. Silence.*)
What's wrong? (*She goes to him and crouches next to him.*)
We're only playing. It's nice to take eggs out. First you look
and look. You're so glad when you find one. And it's nice
when it's still warm…and you can hold it in your hand.
(*Pause.*) Then…there were many eggs. (*Pause.*) Now there's
only one. (*Pause.*) Or maybe two.

FRIKKIE: (*Sadly.*) Ja. (*Suddenly agitated.*) Where is the man?
Why doesn't he come?

SUSSIE: He'll come. You'll see.

FRIKKIE: I hope so. I really hope so.
(*Pause.*)

SUSSIE: Frikkie?

FRIKKIE: Ja?
(*The sound of ALINA rhythmically sweeping the kitchen floor
with a rush broom.*)

SUSSIE: Can I sit on your lap? Please?

FRIKKIE: There's no more time to play.

SUSSIE: Please Boetie. Pleeease. We always play what you
want to! Just the first little bit. Pleeease?

FRIKKIE: No! Leave it now!
(*SUSSIE moves slowly to the bed, dragging her feet. She curls
up on the bed.*)

SUSSIE: (*Speaks to herself. During the next 'Child and Father'
section SUSSIE speaks quietly and fairly rapidly as if she knows
every response by heart. Child's voice.*) Can I ride on Pappie's
foot? Please Pappie? (*Mimicks Father.*) Very well my child.
That's quite enough now. Is Pappie's little girl going to
bed now? (*Child's voice.*) Ja, Pappie. (*Mimicks Father.*) And
what did my little doll do today? (*Child's voice. Sing-song
reciting.*) I gave a little lamb milk, helped old Alina to bake
sweet cakes, and fetched the eggs for Mammie. (*Mimicks
Father.*) That's very good, my child. And what must you

remember to do before you go to sleep? (*Child's voice.*
Sing-song.) Thank you Lord for all my blessings and put my
hands on top of the cover. (*Mimicks Father.*) That's right,
my child. Go to bed now. (*Child's voice.*) Can I get a huggy,
Pappie? (*Mimicks Father.*) Very well, my child. (*Child's voice.*)
Another little kissy? (*Mimicks Father.*) Very well, my child.

FRIKKIE: Stop it! Stop it! Just… (*Faltering.*) stop it.

SUSSIE: What's wrong, Boetie?

FRIKKIE: Nothing. (*He turns his head away. Then he buries his
face in the crook of his arm.*)

SUSSIE: So it's the man, Boetie? Are you scared of the man?
(*Short silence.*)
Come here, Boetie. Come here. We can lie close together.
We can lie 'like birds in a nest'. Warm…and safe. And no
one will see us. No one will find us.
(*FRIKKIE hesitates for a moment. Then he gives a sob and
scrambles onto the bed. He snuggles up to SUSSIE. They put
their arms tightly around each other as the lights fade to black.
In the black, the rhythmic sweeping can still be heard.*)

ACT TWO

As the lights come up, SUSSIE can be seen squatting upstage next to the heap of earth. She is looking down into the excavation. FRIKKIE is moving restlessly about. There is no sound from the kitchen. The tea things have been cleared from the table.

SUSSIE: It's so dark down there. It's deep now.

FRIKKIE: Yes.

SUSSIE: Very deep.

FRIKKIE: Yes. Almost deep enough. It won't be long now. Unless…he stops us. He should have been back by now. How long has he been gone? An hour? Two hours?

SUSSIE: I don't know. Our clock's stopped.

FRIKKIE: What can he be doing? (*Goes to the window.*) What if he got away? What will we do then? (*Opens the curtain.*) I shouldn't have let him go. But I needed time…to make a plan.

SUSSIE: Close the curtains Boetie. I'm frightened. It's so dark out there.

FRIKKIE: There's nothing out there to be frightened of. I've told you!

SUSSIE: (*Turning her face away from the window.*) I'm frightened. Please.

FRIKKIE: Every night it's the same.

SUSSIE: My heart is beating so fast. That's how frightened I am.

FRIKKIE: What are you frightened of? No, I don't want to know. Don't tell me.
(*Short silence.*)

SUSSIE: I'm frightened…

FRIKKIE: I don't want to hear. (*Puts his hands over his ears.*)

SUSSIE: I'm frightened…that I'll see her face! A big face… pressed against the glass!

FRIKKIE: Why do you talk like that?

SUSSIE: Yesterday when it was almost dark, I looked out of the window and I saw Ma standing near the bluegum trees. She was very tall. Taller than the trees.

FRIKKIE: Why do you always lie?

SUSSIE: It's true. And last night when you were sleeping, I heard her nails…scraping against the roof.

FRIKKIE: Stop it! I know you're only trying to frighten me!

SUSSIE: And many times…I can hear her breathing.

FRIKKIE: You know it's just the wind! I told you!

SUSSIE: A cold breath. It makes me shiver. And the curtains flap…and…flap (*Fearful whisper.*) like birds. It's because she's angry.

FRIKKIE: She's dead! They're both dead! Dead and buried in the family graveyard with all the other dead people.

SUSSIE: (*Looks up.*) Maybe…they're up there now. Maybe they're looking at you, Boetie. Watching you. Maybe they can see everything you do.

FRIKKIE: (*Cowering.*) Don't think about that. You must never think about that!

SUSSIE: Pa's big…big…eye in the sky. Burning…like the sun.
(*The sound of a gate opening.*)

FRIKKIE: (*Sitting up.*) Ssh.
(*Footsteps can be heard.*)
(*Very excited.*) There he is. There he is. It's him! Now everything will be all right. You'll see.
(*A knock at the door. FRIKKIE and SUSSIE look at each other. The knock is repeated.*)

GROVÉ: (*Voice off.*) Please open the door! For heaven's sake! It's dark out here!
(*They are doubled up with silent laughter.*)
I know there were things I said! I'm sorry! But please help me! There are jackals out here! Please!

FRIKKIE: I'm busy! I can't open the door! You'll have to go around!

SUSSIE: Ja! To the back door! (*Calling through the window.*) Around here! Be careful! There's a rockery! And don't fall in the old fish-pond!

FRIKKIE: (*Joining her at the window.*) Walk around the big cactus! And remember…there's a water tank on the corner!
(*They run to the kitchen door. Sound of something being kicked over and GROVÉ swearing.*)
Oh! Did you fall over the milk cans? Did you hurt yourself? There's a barbed wire fence! You'll have to climb over!

SUSSIE: Yes! Climb over!

FRIKKIE: Don't step on the cabbages!

SUSSIE: Yes, don't!

FRIKKIE: Or on the pumpkins!

GROVÉ: (*Voice off.*) Ouch!

SUSSIE: (*Excited.*) He walked into the bluegum. He must be close.

ALINA: (*Voice off, complaining.*) A lot of dust!

GROVÉ: (*Voice off.*) I'm sorry, Ousie.[6]

(*GROVÉ appears in the kitchen door. He is dishevelled and covered with dust. He is extremely out of breath.*)

FRIKKIE: (*Lying down on the bed with his hands behind his head.*) So, I thought you never wanted to see us again?

GROVÉ: You should hear them out there. Howling. And the eyes. Shining eyes everywhere. (*Shudders.*) They must be hungry with this drought. (*Pause. FRIKKIE watches him.*) Help me. I'm badly hurt. I'm bleeding. (*Sits down.*) It's my leg. Please look. I...can't stand the sight of blood. (*Closes his eyes and whimpers.*)

(*SUSSIE looks at the cut.*)

Is it bad?

SUSSIE: Quite deep. Not very long.

GROVÉ: Do something. Please.

SUSSIE: Old Alina, bring a cloth! There's lots of blood. Even blood on your shoe.

GROVÉ: What if it won't stop?

(*ALINA brings a cloth.*)

SUSSIE: Just hold it there. Press hard.

GROVÉ: And my clothes are covered in black-jacks.

SUSSIE: Ja. Just look. (*She starts pulling the black-jacks off.*) Were you glad to see our house again?

GROVÉ: Yes...I was.

SUSSIE: When you were far away...did it look very small?

GROVÉ: What?

SUSSIE: The house?

GROVÉ: Yes...it did. (*Groans.*) My leg is throbbing.

---

6 Used in a patronising way when a white person addresses a black woman.

SUSSIE: I used to go to the fields with Pa. It was dark when we came back. And then suddenly I could see the house and all the lights shining in the windows. The house would look so small. And I would think that everything became smaller when we were gone. Chairs, tables, pots... And that now Ma, Alina and Boetie were just as big as (*Looks at a small space between her thumb and forefinger.*) that. (*Laughs. Pulls black-jacks out of GROVÉ's hair.*)

GROVÉ: You're hurting me. Stop! It was terrible out there. Stones and potholes everywhere. And...horrible sounds. Panting...and things...slithering through the grass. And I could hear breathing.

FRIKKIE: We told you.

GROVÉ: (*Lifts the cloth.*) Has it...stopped? Please look.

SUSSIE: (*Looks.*) I think so. Now we can put some ointment on. (*Calling.*) Old Alina...bring some ointment!

GROVÉ: What kind of ointment? I don't want any of those... primitive concoctions.

(*ALINA enters and gives SUSSIE the ointment.*)

SUSSIE: Hold still.

(*SUSSIE applies the ointment.*)

GROVÉ: It burns!

SUSSIE: I'll blow. (*Bends down and blows on the gash.*)

GROVÉ: That's enough. (*Drawing away.*) It feels...better now. (*Short silence.*) Do you think I can have a glass of water? I'm terribly thirsty.

(*ALINA goes back to the kitchen.*)

And once something jumped up right in front of me. I didn't wait to find out what it was. I just...took to my heels. Then I fell over a root...and when I looked up I saw...I was in a graveyard of all things.

FRIKKIE: Five generations of Cilliers are buried there.

SUSSIE: You must never...ever go there. Never...ever.

GROVÉ: I'm not a nervous man... But to be all alone in a place like that. (*Clutches his head.*) I've got a terrible headache. Right here. Behind my eyes.

SUSSIE: Alina could bring you something.

GROVÉ: No...no. It's probably not that bad.

(*ALINA enters with a glass of water.*)

(*Takes the glass from ALINA.*) Thank you ousie. Has it been boiled and filtered?

(*No response. They all watch him. He looks at the water dubiously but then drinks it.*)

And my suit. Just look at it. I've only had it for a week.

(*ALINA takes the empty glass from him and returns to the kitchen.*)

SUSSIE: We'll look after you. My Ma taught me to be nice to guests. (*Whispers meaningfully.*) Never ever.

(*Short silence. GROVÉ looks completely despairing. He drops his head in his hands.*)

GROVÉ: (*Brokenly.*) My wife will be waiting for me. I know how she worries.

(*Short silence.*)

SUSSIE: Then you're going to stay?

GROVÉ: Well, miss…if I may…just…until the sun rises.

SUSSIE: Ja! Ja! (*Coy.*) but don't just sit there. Make yourself at home. (*Pleased.*) You can sleep on the bed with me! It's nice and soft. (*Picks up the pillow and holds it against her.*) My pillow is hard and flat but this one still has all its feathers…

FRIKKIE: That's my pillow! You're not giving him my pillow!

SUSSIE: All right! All right!

(*FRIKKIE grabs the pillow and clutches it. He lies down on the bed again.*)

(*Smiling graciously.*) 'Only the best for a guest.' That's what Ma used to say. (*Suddenly excited.*) I know! I know! (*She rushes to the chest and opens it. Rummaging in the chest.*) Pa's pillow! He's dead, so you can use it. And a blanket! (*She finds the pillow and holds it out to him. The pillow has rust coloured stains on it.*)

GROVÉ: Really, miss, I don't need a pillow…

FRIKKIE: Take the pillow!

GROVÉ: Very well!

(*Taking the pillow very gingerly. Pause. He looks at FRIKKIE. SUSSIE closes the chest with a loud thud.*)

If you insist. (*He puts the pillow on the bed and wipes his hands on his trousers.*)

SUSSIE: You see, I told you. We know how to treat our guests, don't we Boet?

(Silence. FRIKKIE doesn't answer. He is still lying on the bed and staring at GROVÉ. SUSSIE shakes out the blanket.)

GROVÉ: *(Clearing his throat and moving to the foot of the bed.)* Mr Cilliers... I want to tell you...how sorry I am about what I said before I left. It was very...unprofessional of me.

FRIKKIE: Ja.

(While GROVÉ continues to speak, SUSSIE sings the Afrikaans folk song Siembamba[7] in a soft, high, tuneless way as she arranges the blanket on the bench.
GROVÉ and SUSSIE together.)

GROVÉ: It's just...well...to tell you the truth... I can't understand why you won't be more sensible... What are you trying to say? You see... Miss Cilliers put all her affairs into my hands. And I think we can come to a...sensible agreement. We don't want this...to drag on.

SUSSIE: 'Siembamba, mother's sweetheart Siembamba, mother's sweetheart.' 'Wring his neck and jump on his head.' 'Throw him in a ditch and then he's dead.' *(She continues to hum the tune.)*

FRIKKIE: Like what?

SUSSIE: *(Standing back to admire her handiwork. Very loudly in Mother's voice.)* Alina!! There will be a guest for dinner! *(With a bright, artificial smile to GROVÉ. Still Mother's voice.)* Dinner will soon be served, Mr Grové.

GROVÉ: *(Confused.)* Thank you. *(To FRIKKIE.)* Why not sell this farm Mr Cilliers? Why not sell? I mean...take this house for instance. *(Looks around.)* Just look at the cracks! They're so big that you can see right through them! *(ALINA enters with a tray. On the tray there is cutlery and crockery. SUSSIE runs to her excitedly.)*

SUSSIE: *(Little child sing-song voice.)* Can I help? Can I help you, old Alina? Can I help you, old Alina?

---

7 A bitter song referring to the children dying in the concentration camps during the Anglo-Boer war.

ALINA: (*Kindly.*) The nonnie, she can help me.
 (*SUSSIE helps ALINA to lay the table.*)
GROVÉ: One of these days, it's going to collapse, mark
 my words. Yes, that's what will happen to you: dead and
 buried under the rubble.
 (*FRIKKIE stares at him without reacting.*)
 And out there! There's nothing out there! Nothing! I've
 never seen...such desolation.
ALINA: (*Angrily.*) Nonna! The spoon! You put it wrong!
SUSSIE: (*Snivelling.*) I'm sorry old Alina.
 (*FRIKKIE gets up from the bed and moves to GROVÉ. He
 stands very close to GROVÉ.*)
FRIKKIE: (*Softly and ominously.*) Let me tell you something.
 I sit here and I wait for the rain. The rain doesn't come.
 But I wait here. Here – where I belong. I wait and I wait
 and every day the sun burns deeper into me. It burns
 through my skin. It burns through my flesh. It burns...into
 my bones. But...I wait. (*Loudly.*) And I'll always be here!
 Because this is my place!!
SUSSIE: (*Very loudly. Mother's voice.*) Dinner is served!
GROVÉ: (*Moving towards the table.*) Well...if you feel so
 strongly about the matter...but I think you're making a big
 mistake... (*He sits.*)
FRIKKIE: He's taking my chair!
SUSSIE: (*Own voice.*) Sit on the paraffin tin! (*Mother's voice to
 GROVÉ.*) You'll have to share our simple meal with us, Mr
 Grové. You see, we weren't expecting any guests.
 (*ALINA enters with three bowls of soup on a tray. And puts
 them on the table. FRIKKIE tastes the soup, burns his mouth
 and starts – noisily – to blow on the soup.*)
GROVÉ: (*Taking a fly out of the soup.*) I'm sure it will be very
 tasty, miss.
SUSSIE: (*Looking at FRIKKIE. Mother's voice.*) Frederik! Aren't
 you going to say grace?
FRIKKIE: (*Mutters. Shy.*) Sorry...
 (*They all close their eyes.*)
SUSSIE: (*Mother's voice.*) Frederik! I'm waiting!
FRIKKIE: (*Mutters very rapidly.*) Dear Lord, for what we are
 about to receive, make us truly thankful.

GROVÉ: (*Tentatively starting to eat.*) I can see that you are still
faithful to the traditions of our forefathers. That is very
good.

SUSSIE: (*Own voice.*) Ja. We do everything they did. But not
the sjambok[8].

GROVÉ: The sjambok, miss?

SUSSIE: Yes. The sjambok. We don't use that any more.
Look! There it hangs on the door!

GROVÉ: (*Looking.*) Oh yes. I see.
(*While they are talking, FRIKKIE is busy eating noisily.*)

SUSSIE: My grandpa used it. And my Pa used it. But we
don't use it any more. (*Silence while they eat. Leaning forward
confidentially.*) Pa was a strict man, meneer. Strict but just,
that's what he always said. (*Giggling.*) When Frikkie was
naughty Pa would say, 'Come here, my son.' And then
Frikkie went slowly down the passage to his room with Pa
just behind him hurrying him up and saying, 'Come, come,
come,' then Pa closed the door. (*Secretively.*) And I always
sat near the door to listen.

FRIKKIE: Come now Sussie. I'm sure…

SUSSIE: It was always quiet. Quiet in the room. And then
I could hear the sjambok whistling through the air and
smacking down on Boetie's buttocks. (*Confidential.*) Because
– you see – he had to pull his pants down first.

FRIKKIE: Sussie! Stop it!

SUSSIE: I'll talk if I want to! It used to go on like that for a
long time. The whistling sound…and then the smacking
sound. Ja. But he never cried. No. Never. Not Frikkie. But
when Pa left the room I used to go in softly and he would
be lying on the bed…on his stomach. And I would say,
'Boetie,' and he would say, 'Go away, Sussie… Go away.'
Always the same. (*Suddenly concerned.*) You mustn't think
badly of Pa. It was for his own good. Frikkie's. Because you
see, Pa had to make a man of him.
(*FRIKKIE is sitting with his head down.*)

GROVÉ: Not at all, miss. I understand only too well. I also
have a little boy of my own and this little man – small as
he is – already knows the difference between right and

8 A short whip.

wrong. Ja-nee, there's only one thing a child understands. (*Short silence.*) This vegetable soup is very good. Really very good.

SUSSIE: But not me! Never! Pa would never lift his hand against a woman. When I was naughty, I had to write out the commandments. One thousand times. (*Very fast.*) Thou shalt not kill thy neighbour or his ox or his wife. Honour they mother and father…

FRIKKIE: Stop it!!

GROVÉ: (*Pushing his plate away.*) I always say there's nothing like a good hot plate of vegetable soup.

SUSSIE: Would you like some more?

GROVÉ: (*Hastily.*) No thank you. I've done very well. (*FRIKKIE burps loudly.*)

SUSSIE: (*Mother's voice, very loud.*) Alina! Come and clear the table.

GROVÉ: So…you say the neighbouring farm is about three miles from here?

FRIKKIE: About.

(*SUSSIE sees a mosquito and follows its movements with her eyes.*)

GROVÉ: I'll have to be on my way very early tomorrow morning.

(*ALINA enters with the tray and starts clearing the table. SUSSIE kills the mosquito by clapping her palms together.*)

FRIKKIE: You mustn't do that! If they smell the blood, then more will come.

SUSSIE: (*Studies her palm. Own voice.*) It's full of blood! (*Pause. She looks up slowly.*) Is it mine…or yours…or Alina's… (*They all look at GROVÉ.*) Or is it his?

GROVÉ: (*Uneasy. Speaking too loudly.*) Would you please wake me up early tomorrow morning, Mr Cilliers? What time do you get up?

FRIKKIE: About five or six o'clock.

GROVÉ: That suits me very well.

FRIKKIE: In the afternoon.

GROVÉ: But you can't be serious! I mean… Well, a boer should get up bright and early. There's work to be done!

You won't get anywhere if you sleep all day. There must be something you can do to save the situation! How can you sleep…while everything around you is going to ruin?!

SUSSIE: (*Whining.*) Don't be angry with us. Don't be angry.

GROVÉ: Come now, miss! Stop behaving like this! Pull yourself together! (*Shouting.*) Stop behaving like a child! You're a grown woman! I wish you could see yourself! Your behaviour is completely ridiculous!

(*SUSSIE crawls under the table. She buries her head in her arms and makes small – almost animal-like – sounds of distress.*)

ALINA: (*Appearing in the kitchen door.*) Jona[9], my Nonnie! Jona! (*Goes to the table and bends down.*) Tula[10], Nonnie. Tula… tula…Nonnie.

(*SUSSIE gives a soft cry, then puts her arms around ALINA's neck and gets on her back. ALINA keeps saying, 'Tula shoo shoo,' etc. As she goes to the kitchen with SUSSIE on her back. SUSSIE is still whimpering. FRIKKIE follows them to the kitchen.*)

FRIKKIE: (*In the kitchen.*) There now, Sussie. There now. Don't cry.

(*SUSSIE still cries softly. GROVÉ sits down on the bed and wipes his glasses. After a while FRIKKIE comes back into the room. He is carrying a long rope. He goes to the window and looks out while he knots the rope. SUSSIE can be heard softly whimpering in the kitchen while ALINA sings a soothing, monotonous Sotho song.*)

GROVÉ: (*Mildly.*) I'm sorry… I know I'm only a guest in your house…

FRIKKIE: (*Ominous.*) You made my sister cry.

GROVÉ: But I'm only trying to help.

FRIKKIE: (*Turning to him, suddenly violent.*) You made my sister cry!

GROVÉ: I'm sorry…but I was just trying to show you. I mean…an honest day's work has never done anyone any harm… On the contrary…

FRIKKIE: Are you saying we don't work? We work hard. Yes. And you say we do nothing?

---

9 A Sotho word, used to express alarm.

10 A Sotho word meaning 'hush'.

GROVÉ: (*Humouring him.*) How can you work? When you sleep all day? Tell me that!

FRIKKIE: (*Triumphant.*) We work all night!

GROVÉ: (*Shaking his head.*) In the night. And what kind of 'work' do you do at night?

FRIKKIE: (*Inspired.*) Good work! Rescue work! We work to save our farm!

GROVÉ: (*Wearily.*) What can you be talking about?

FRIKKIE: We've been waiting for the rain, ja. We've been waiting a long time. But it never comes. This farm is cursed. Dust in our eyes, in our mouths, in our ears. Choking us. And it never comes. But (*Softly and mysteriously.*) the water doesn't just fall from up there… It also…rises up…from deep, deep under the earth.
(*SUSSIE appears in the kitchen door.*)

GROVÉ: Oh please. If you're talking about that little trickle you use to water your vegetable garden, then I'm afraid… I'd better get some sleep. You can't perhaps provide me with pyjamas? I would be very grateful.

SUSSIE: You can use Pa's. (*Moves towards the chest.*)
(*FRIKKIE moves to the mound of earth.*)

GROVÉ: You see…I don't want to get my clothes creased.

FRIKKIE: No. I'm not talking about a…trickle of water.

SUSSIE: (*Taking a pair of striped pyjamas from the chest.*) Here!

FRIKKIE: I'm talking about an underground river! Swollen with rushing, black water!

SUSSIE: Take it.

GROVÉ: Thank you, miss.

FRIKKIE: I know it's there. I can hear it. I can smell it. The clean, cold, shining water!

GROVÉ: (*Taking the toothbrush from his briefcase.*) At least I brought a toothbrush, miss. I'm never without one. (*He takes a minute tube of toothpaste from his briefcase.*) Where is the bathroom?

SUSSIE: (*Indicating.*) Over there.
(*GROVÉ goes to the washroom.*)

FRIKKIE: (*Loudly, so that GROVÉ can hear.*) When it became cool and dark…I used to go out with my willow branch!

(*GROVÉ can be heard brushing his teeth in the washroom. SUSSIE sits on the bed and listens – entranced – to FRIKKIE's story.*)

I walked and walked but I never found any water! One evening I came home! I still had the branch in my hands when I suddenly felt it bending! I held it tightly and it pulled and pulled…like a big fish on a line! And just there – where Ma's harmonium used to stand – I crouched down with my ear to the ground. And then I heard it!

SUSSIE: He did! Yes he did!

(*GROVÉ gargles and spits.*)

FRIKKIE: The rushing of water! It made me dizzy!

GROVÉ: (*Voice off, from washroom.*) Well, even if it is as you say, you can't afford to drill. It's very expensive, you know.

(*FRIKKIE and SUSSIE look at each other.*)

FRIKKIE: We don't have to drill.

SUSSIE: No. We dig!

GROVÉ: (*Appearing in the door.*) Dig?

FRIKKIE: Ja.

SUSSIE: Ja! So you see we have our work! (*Points to mound of earth.*) There's our work. Every evening when it gets cooler…then we work. Sometimes we work all night.

(*SUSSIE goes to the mound and crouches next to FRIKKIE.*)

FRIKKIE: And as we dig and dig…it gets louder. The rushing sound.

SUSSIE: Ja. Like the humming of many bees…or tall trees in the wind. Oh, you must come and hear it. Please. Just come and listen.

GROVÉ: (*Who is neatly arranging his pants, shirt and jacket over a chair.*) Really miss…

SUSSIE: Pleeease. Pleeease.

GROVÉ: Oh, very well. (*GROVÉ moves to the mound of earth, bends down and pretends to listen. Silence while they all listen. Getting up.*) I'm sorry…but I don't hear anything. (*Humouring them.*) Maybe I don't have your acute hearing. (*FRIKKIE and SUSSIE don't react. They are enraptured as they listen. GROVÉ takes a handkerchief from his jacket pocket and spreads it carefully on the pillow before he gets into bed. He lies on the very edge of the bed with his face to the audience. He takes off his glasses and puts them on the floor next to him.)*

SUSSIE: One of these days, the water will come spurting out. I know it will! A shining fountain.

FRIKKIE: And we'll close all the doors…

SUSSIE: And all the windows…

FRIKKIE: And the house will fill with water!

SUSSIE: Rooms like caves!

FRIKKIE: We'll grow…scales…and fins.

SUSSIE: And we'll swim around like fish!

(FRIKKIE makes fast, gliding movements as he opens and shuts his mouth in a fish-like way. SUSSIE laughs.)

GROVÉ: *(Sitting up.)* Please! Please! You've lost all touch with reality! Things cannot go on like this!

(They look at GROVÉ.)

FRIKKIE: What are you trying to say?

GROVÉ: I was just…well, to tell the truth, Mr Cilliers, I think you and your sister are both a little…

FRIKKIE: Ja?

GROVÉ: A little tired.

FRIKKIE: Tired?

GROVÉ: Yes. That's what I wanted to say. It must be… *(Indicating the mound.)* all the work. Yes, that must be it. *(Glib.)* And personally I feel that you need some rest. It would do you both the world of good to get away for a while.

SUSSIE: *(Snivelling.)* Does he want to send us away, Boet?

GROVÉ: *(Very friendly.)* It doesn't have to be for long. Just until you…feel better. Rested. In fact, I know of just the place. Big grounds, tennis courts, and nice people…to take care of you. I'll make all the arrangements. Just leave it to me.

FRIKKIE: We're not going anywhere, Mr Grové.

GROVÉ: But you can't stay here. This situation…can only get worse.

SUSSIE: Why can't we stay here, Boetie? Why not? Does he want to…spoil everything?

FRIKKIE: Ja, Sussie. He wants to.

SUSSIE: And what now, Boet?

FRIKKIE: Leave it Sussie. It's getting late. We must go to bed.

GROVÉ: (*Relieved.*) I completely agree. (*He lies down.*)

SUSSIE: But Boetie…he's spoiling everything…

FRIKKIE: (*Stripping down to his underwear.*) Forget about it, Sussie!

SUSSIE: He wants to spoil everything…

GROVÉ: (*Pulling the blanket up to his chin.*) Please don't upset yourself, miss. It was only a suggestion.

SUSSIE: (*Angry.*) And why must we sleep because he wants to? We have to work! We always work when it's dark!

FRIKKIE: I'm telling you to go to sleep! There'll be trouble if you don't!

ALINA: (*Appearing in the kitchen doorway.*) Why you fight?

SUSSIE: Frikkie wants me to go to sleep…and I don't want to.

ALINA: (*Sternly.*) Come now, Nonnie. If the basie say you must sleep, you must sleep.

(*FRIKKIE goes to the washroom. The sound of someone urinating noisily into a bucket.*)

Come. You must take off the clothes now, Nonnie. Come Nonnie…lift the arms.

(*ALINA helps SUSSIE to take off her dress. ALINA picks the crumpled night-dress up from the floor and helps SUSSIE to put it on as FRIKKIE enters and lies down on the bench.*)

GROVÉ: (*Lifting his head.*) Excuse me… Could your Ousie wake me up? What time does she get up?

FRIKKIE: Why don't you ask her?

ALINA: Now Nonnie…you must climb in the bed.

GROVÉ: (*As though speaking to an idiot.*) Ousie…tomorrow early…you must…wake…me…up. Do you understand?

SUSSIE: Boetie…I'm too shy to pray in front of him.

FRIKKIE: Forget the praying and sleep.

SUSSIE: But Ma said I must never go to sleep like a heathen.

GROVÉ: Ousie! I'm talking to you!

(*ALINA turns and looks at him.*)

Can…you…understand? Wake…me…up!

ALINA: (*Muttering under her breath.*) Au! Sooka!

GROVÉ: (*To ALINA.*) I heard that! What did you say? I'm talking to you! (*To SUSSIE and FRIKKIE.*) What did she say to me? (*To ALINA.*) You'd better watch out! Do you hear me?

(*ALINA blows out the lamp next to the bed and the lamp on the table. She moves towards the kitchen.*)

(*Desperately.*) Ousie!

(*ALINA turns and looks at him.*)

Please! Wake…me…up. (*Rubbing his thumb and forefinger together.*) I'll give you something. Give…you…something.

(*ALINA turns and goes back into the kitchen. GROVÉ sighs and lies down.*)

SUSSIE: Goodnight. Goodnight Boetie.

FRIKKIE: (*Yawning.*) Goodnight Sussie.

(*There is a lamp burning in the kitchen and the flickering shadows on the kitchen wall indicate ALINA's movement. While there is silence in the room, there are noises from the kitchen. The silence in the room continues for some time.*)

SUSSIE: (*Suddenly sitting up and wailing.*) Boetie! Boetiiie!

FRIKKIE: What is it?

SUSSIE: He touched me!

FRIKKIE: (*Sitting up.*) What do you mean?

SUSSIE: (*Crying.*) He touched me Boetie… He touched me…there.

FRIKKIE: Where?

(*GROVÉ sits up and looks bewildered.*)

SUSSIE: I can't tell you. Ma said I should never talk about… that.

FRIKKIE: You mean there?

SUSSIE: Ja…a…a

GROVÉ: I assure you…

(*FRIKKIE jumps up, goes to the bed and drags GROVÉ onto the floor.*)

FRIKKIE: (*Crouching over GROVÉ and banging his head on the floor.*) What have you done to my sister?

GROVÉ: Please! I didn't do anything!

FRIKKIE: You filthy…disgusting…filthy…pig!

GROVÉ: I didn't touch anything!

FRIKKIE: You animal!

(*FRIKKIE picks GROVÉ up from the floor and pushes him towards the bench.*)

You don't come near my sister again, do you understand?

GROVÉ: Yes. I promise. But please… I didn't do anything.

FRIKKIE: Lie down!

GROVÉ: (*Lying down on the bench and pulling the blanket up to his chin.*) All I did was to scratch a little… There are so many fleas…

FRIKKIE: (*Pulling the pillow from under his head, whining, almost childish.*) That's my pillow!

(*He takes the pillow and gets into bed next to SUSSIE who is still snivelling.*)

SUSSIE: Boetie…can I lie in your arm?

FRIKKIE: Ja Sussie.

(*SUSSIE snuggles up to FRIKKIE. Silence. There are shadows on the kitchen wall as ALINA moves about. Slight intensification of African night sounds.*

FRIKKIE whispers and SUSSIE giggles.

Silence.

They whisper.

Silence.

SUSSIE giggles loudly.)

GROVÉ: (*Whining.*) Please… Please… Let me get some sleep at least.

(*FRIKKIE and SUSSIE giggle. Then there is a fairly long silence. Night sounds. ALINA chopping vegetables in the kitchen. After a time, GROVÉ starts snoring lightly. As the snoring continues, FRIKKIE sits up and listens intently. Then he strikes a match and lights the lamp next to the bed. SUSSIE whispers and he replies in a whisper. He gets up slowly while he watches GROVÉ. He walks to the table and lights the lamp on the table. He picks up the rope lying in front of the window. He picks up his shorts from the floor, takes a pocket knife from the pocket and cuts the rope into two pieces. SUSSIE watches him intently.*)

FRIKKIE: (*Whispering.*) Come on…

(*SUSSIE gets out of bed, runs to FRIKKIE and takes a piece of rope from him. FRIKKIE whispers softly and indicates towards GROVÉ's feet.*)

(*Slightly louder.*) …and make a double knot.

SUSSIE: (*Whispering.*) Like the last time?

FRIKKIE: (*Whispering.*) Ja. Are you ready?

SUSSIE: (*Whispering loudly.*) Ja!

GROVÉ: (*Sits bolt upright and strains to see without his glasses.*)
And now? What's going on?

FRIKKIE: (*Hiding the rope behind his back.*) I…heard a noise.

GROVÉ: A noise?

FRIKKIE: Ja. A noise. (*Inspired.*) A scratching at the back door!
(*SUSSIE hides her rope behind her back.*)

GROVÉ: I told you! I told you they were out there! (*Looking around.*) And what about the window? The glass is broken.
They can get in through the window.

FRIKKIE: I'm not scared of a jackal. I'll go and see. (*He pretends to go into the kitchen, but stands in the door and watches GROVÉ.*)
(*GROVÉ sighs and lies down. He tosses and turns.*)
(*Whisper.*) If only he'd…lie still.

SUSSIE: Mister… Mister…

GROVÉ: (*Sighing and pulling the blanket up to his chin.*) Don't be afraid. Your brother knows what to do.
(*SUSSIE moves to the bench and stands at its foot, leaning over GROVÉ.*)
Keep away from me! You know what your brother said.

SUSSIE: But…

FRIKKIE: Sussie! Be quiet! Mr Grové wants to sleep.

GROVÉ: That's right. I have a long day tomorrow.

SUSSIE: I just wanted to say, mister…

GROVÉ: (*Sighs.*) What is it?

SUSSIE: If you…close your eyes…and lie very…very quietly…then I'll tell you a story.

GROVÉ: That won't be necessary.

SUSSIE: A very nice story.

GROVÉ: Will you be quiet then? Do you promise?

SUSSIE: I will.

GROVÉ: Very well. (*Sighs.*) I hope it's not too long.

SUSSIE: But close your eyes. And you mustn't move. (*She stands at the foot of the bed.*) One night it was very hot. I was trying to sleep but there were too many mosquitoes and there was a big moth…banging against the ceiling. Then I heard a voice at the window. I got out of bed and went to look. It was Boetie. I looked out and saw him. He was standing in the flower-bed looking up at me. And just…just above his head was the biggest moon I've ever seen. He was calling me to come and play. And do you know what he wanted us to play? 'Boetie and Sussie send Pa and Ma away.' And after we played it, they were gone and they never came back.

(*While SUSSIE has been talking, FRIKKIE has moved stealthily to the head of GROVÉ's bed.*)

GROVÉ: Is that the story?

SUSSIE: Yes.

GROVÉ: Funny story. It makes no sense.

SUSSIE: But…it's true.

GROVÉ: What do you mean…true?

SUSSIE: They scolded us. Yes, they did! And…and…they wanted…to change everything. Just like you.

GROVÉ: (*Desperately.*) Please. Can't we talk about this in the morning? You said you'd be quiet.

FRIKKIE: That's just the end. Why don't we tell you the whole story? From the beginning.

GROVÉ: I'm aching all over. I think I'm getting a fever. Please just let me rest! I beg you!
(*Short silence.*)

FRIKKIE: There was a big storm. It was dark outside. Everything was shaking…and trembling. Crashes of thunder.

SUSSIE: And flashes of lightning.

FRIKKIE: Sussie was scared.

SUSSIE: Yes. I'm scared of storms. I got up and went to Boetie's bed. We held each other and then we slept. Listening to the rain. (*Smiles tenderly.*)

FRIKKIE: But Ma was coming down the passage. Creeping quietly.
(*Sharp intake of breath from SUSSIE.*)
And even in our sleep…we could feel her getting closer. And in our dreams we could see her opening the door… quietly…quietly…because the hinges creaked. I woke up because I heard something, but I thought it must be a mouse…or a cricket. But it was her…coming closer. Creeping softly…very softly. And then she was standing at the foot of the bed…looking at us.

SUSSIE: I woke up because I could feel her eyes… Her
eyes…hurting me. She was holding a candle…with a thin,
sharp flame.
(*Suddenly, without warning, SUSSIE assumes the grown-up
persona. She becomes rigid, her gaze transfixed on the bed. At
first she addresses an imaginary SUSSIE lying on the left side
and then an imaginary FRIKKIE on the right.*)
(*Mother's voice, loud.*) Damnation! You will burn in hell!
Yes. Burn in hell! And shame! You have brought shame
on our family! (*To 'Sussie'.*) Always so quiet. Always so
good. 'Pappie's little doll.' But I should have known! You
will be sent away. You will not spend another day near
your brother. (*To 'Frikkie'.*) And you! Your father will flay
you alive! Flay you alive! (*Gasping for breath.*) You are
not my children! No! I have not given birth to such…
monstrosities! Spawn of the Devil! How have I sinned?
What have I done…to deserve…this? (*Own voice.*) And…
then they locked us up… We stayed there all day. Without
any food.
FRIKKIE: Each in our own room… Waiting to be punished.
SUSSIE: I couldn't sleep… And then you knocked on the
window.
FRIKKIE: Ja. (*Smiling dreamily.*) It was a warm night and
outside it smelled of wet earth. I said, 'Come Sussie…
come,' and I helped you to climb through the window.
SUSSIE: And when we got to Ma and Pa's window…it was
open. You lifted me through and then you climbed in after
me.
FRIKKIE: Pa was lying on his back. He was snoring.
SUSSIE: Ma was lying on her side…with her hands under her
cheek.
FRIKKIE: (*Quietly.*) And…they never scolded us again.
SUSSIE: No, they didn't. (*To GROVÉ, soft and confidential.*) You
see mister…that's how we played it. (*She takes the rope from
under her pillow.*)
GROVÉ: (*Sitting up slowly and blinking.*) What do you mean? I
don't understand.
(*SUSSIE runs lightly to front left. She crouches down and knocks
on the floor.*)

SUSSIE: Here's Pa's right hand. His big strong hand. (*She runs to front right and does the same.*) And here are Ma's sharp eyes. (*Little laugh.*) 'Boetie and Sussie put Ma and Pa away.' We play it almost every day. It's our best game. (*Confiding.*) Ma used to say this was a vale of sorrows. We sent them to a better place.

GROVÉ: (*Shocked.*) You're really going too far. This game is in very poor taste.

(*SUSSIE takes the rope from behind her back and moves towards GROVÉ. FRIKKIE gives her a sign.*)

SUSSIE: It's the truth. Cross my heart and hope to die. They wanted to spoil everything...like you... And they scolded us...like you. You shouldn't have done that. That was wrong. I told you so. Didn't I?

(*SUSSIE jumps onto GROVÉ's legs and ties his ankles together, while FRIKKIE slips a noose around his neck and ties his arms close to his body with the other end of the rope. While they tie him up they speak almost simultaneously.*)

(*Sing-song.*) Ja, ja, just like with Pa. Ja, ja.

FRIKKIE: I told you... I warned you...but you wouldn't listen!

GROVÉ: No! No! What are you doing? Leave me alone! You're hurting me! Stop this at once!

FRIKKIE: Sussie! The sjambok!

(*SUSSIE runs to the door and takes the sjambok from the nail, while GROVÉ is thrashing about and protesting wildly.*)

(*To SUSSIE.*) And the hat! (*To GROVÉ.*) Lie still!

(*SUSSIE takes their father's hat from another nail and runs to FRIKKIE with the hat and the sjambok.*)

SUSSIE: (*Putting the hat on GROVÉ's head.*) There Boet!

GROVÉ: Please...please...if this is one of your games... then I don't want to play!

FRIKKIE: (*Father's voice.*) And what happened to the sheets? Tell me!

GROVÉ: The sheets?

FRIKKIE: (*Father's voice.*) I hear you've messed on the sheets again. That's true, isn't it?

GROVÉ: No! I don't know anything about sheets! Please! I swear to you!

FRIKKIE: (*Father's voice.*) Don't lie to me! He did mess on the sheets again, isn't that true, my wife.

SUSSIE: (*Mother's voice.*) Ja, my husband. It is true.

GROVÉ: Please! I don't know what you're talking about!

FRIKKIE: Come you little runt! You're no son of mine!
(*FRIKKIE pulls GROVÉ up from the bench and starts dragging him towards the kitchen. GROVÉ has to hop like a rabbit.*)

GROVÉ: (*Falling down.*) I don't know anything about sheets!

FRIKKIE: Get up!

SUSSIE: (*Clapping her hands, very excited.*) Pull him, Boetie! Pull him!

GROVÉ: Help! Help! Someone help me! Ousie! Ousie! Help me!

FRIKKIE: (*Near the kitchen door. Calling to ALINA in the kitchen.*) Come old Alina! Help me! We must hang him from the meat-hook! By his heels.

GROVÉ: (*Beside himself.*) Aaah…aah…please…help!!
(*FRIKKIE pushes him into the kitchen. SUSSIE stays at the door and watches with relish.*)

FRIKKIE: (*Voice off, from kitchen.*) Be quiet! You'll get what you deserve! You'll remember this thrashing for the rest of your life! You're filthy! Filthy!
(*SUSSIE crouches at the door and watches.*)

GROVÉ: (*Voice off, from the kitchen.*) Help! What are you doing! (*Some muffled screams.*) No! I have a child! Help! Don't hurt me! Please! Help! Help! (*Incoherent sounds of terror.*)

SUSSIE: Pull his pants down, Boetie! Pull them down!
(*The sjambok whistles through the air and smacks down on GROVÉ's buttocks. Each time this happens there is a blood-curdling scream. With each cut of the sjambok, SUSSIE's body jerks with an almost erotic excitement. After about fifteen cuts, GROVÉ only whimpers and after a few more cuts he is silent.*)
(*Still crouching.*) He doesn't complain any more, does he Boet?
(*Another cut.*)
Now he's good, isn't he Boet?
(*Another cut.*)
(*Getting up to have a better look.*) Shoe. There's a lot of blood

Boet. (*Suddenly excited.*) Hey, Boet! What does he remind you of? Guess Boet. Come on, just guess.

(*ALINA enters. She takes the blanket from the bench and folds it. Another cut.*

As SUSSIE continues to talk, ALINA also folds GROVÉ's clothes very carefully. She opens the chest. She puts the clothes and the blanket into the chest and closes it with a thud.)

(*Triumphant.*) He looks like one of the springbok that Ma used to skin when she made biltong![11] And the buck used to hang just like that. Upside down! And the blood...the blood would drip into the white enamel bath...for a whole day.

(*Another cut. ALINA exits to the kitchen.*)

Ja, you could hear it. Drip...drip...drip...

(*Silence. She crouches down again.*

FRIKKIE comes into the room. His vest is splattered with blood. He hangs the sjambok and the hat back on the door and then stumbles to the bed. He is breathing heavily and obviously exhausted. He sits on the bed and wipes the blood from his arms and neck with a dirty dishcloth. SUSSIE sits very still and watches him. After a while, FRIKKIE starts to snivel. He wipes his nose with the back of his hand. SUSSIE gets up and walks slowly towards him. She sits next to him and puts her arm around his shoulders. They sit together in silence.)

(*Gently.*) One of these days Boetie...ja...you'll see...one of these days the water will come out, and it will stream through the house...and wash everything away... Ma's church dress and Pa's shoes...the sjambok...the feather pillows...the bed...everything. You'll see Boetie. You'll see! And...big plants will grow...with broad leaves. And flowers! Ja! Green...and flowers everywhere. Big, big flowers. Turning...like windmills.

(*FRIKKIE turns his head and looks at her.*)

(*Gently, coaxing.*) Do you want to work now, Boet? We can if you want to.

FRIKKIE: No. I'm too tired tonight.

SUSSIE: So what do you want to do, Frikkie?

11 Partially dried strips of raw meat, a traditional Afrikaner delicacy.

71

FRIKKIE: I don't know. I think I want to sleep.

SUSSIE: Ja. That's right. We must sleep. (*She goes to the kitchen door. Timidly.*) Alina...old Alina... We want to go to bed now.

(*ALINA appears in the door. She is wiping her hands on her apron.*)

ALINA: (*Kindly.*) Come, Nonna. (*She takes SUSSIE by the arm and leads her to the bed.*)

SUSSIE: (*Kneeling down with her eyes closed and her hands folded.*) Gentle Jesus, meek and mild, look upon this little child. Amen.

(*ALINA takes the dishcloth from FRIKKIE and helps him into bed. SUSSIE gets into bed and ALINA tucks them in.*)

ALINA: Nonnie...Basie... You must sleep very nice. (*She blows out the lamp next to the bed.*)

SUSSIE: Night, Alina.

FRIKKIE: Night, Alina.

(*ALINA goes to the washroom and blows out the lamp. Then she crosses to the table and blows out the lamp on the table before she exits towards the kitchen.*
Short silence.)

SUSSIE: It's dark, Boetie.

FRIKKIE: Yes.

(*Short silence.*)

SUSSIE: Can you hear them, Boetie?

FRIKKIE: Sussie...you mustn't.

SUSSIE: They want to get in. They want me to open the windows and the doors. They can't do it by themselves.

FRIKKIE: But...you won't.

SUSSIE: No, I won't. I promise.

(*Short silence.*)

What do you think, Boetie? Are they still the same...or have they changed?

FRIKKIE: Maybe they've changed. Maybe they're... different now.

(*Short silence.*)

SUSSIE: They're waiting for us, Boetie. Out there. (*She sits up.*) They're waiting for us.

(*FRIKKIE gives a choking sob.*)

FRIKKIE: (*Calling.*) Alina! Alina!
>   (*ALINA appears in the kitchen door and looks at him.*)
>   Don't leave us, old Alina…

SUSSIE: Ja, old Alina. We're scared…

FRIKKIE: Stay with us, old Alina.

SUSSIE: Just until we sleep. (*Lies down again.*)
>   (*ALINA shakes her head and clicks her tongue fondly. Then she moves slowly to the downstage side of the bed. She sits on the floor. The room is in darkness except for the faint bar of light coming from the kitchen door. She sings a slow, soothing Sotho lullaby. She repeats the song as the lights slowly fade to black.*)
>   Eou eou eou
>   Eou eou eou
>   Tula tula tula
>   Tula tula tula
>   Etse ke etela
>   Mphorane ngoana' me
>   Ka fumana ngoana mokhotse
>   A kula ngoana me
>   Eou eou eou
>   Eou eou eou
>   Tula tula tula
>   Tula tula tula
>   Eou eou eou
>   Tula tula tula
>   Tula tula tula[12]

12 The words of the lullaby are in Sotho and mean: 'You are lost children who have wandered far away from home. Now you are in a strange place. But I will look after you and comfort you.'

GOOD HEAVENS

Characters

MA
a frail, elderly woman. She wears
a night-cap and a night-dress

SOPHIE
her stepdaughter. Thirty-eight, pale and bony with her
sparse hair dragged back into a small, tight bun. She is
somberly and plainly dressed. At the start of the play
she is wearing a calico apron

MINNIE
her other stepdaughter. Thirty-six, pasty faced and
dwarfish. Badly dressed with her thin, oily hair folded
into a hair-net

TOMMIE
their half-brother, son of Ma. A fresh-faced, mild man
of about thirty. He has the innocence and mental age of
a child of ten

BABY
his sister, half-sister to Sophie and Minnie. A sweet
young girl wearing a simple white dress

Accent
These characters are not English-speaking South
Africans, but Afrikaners and as such a 'South African'
accent is not required. 'Normal' English can be used,
since the convention is that the characters are speaking
Afrikaans.

The original version of this play, *Op Dees Aarde*, was first staged in 1986 by the ATKV in the Breytenbach Theatre in Pretoria, directed by Denys Webb. The first professional production of this play was staged in 1987 by PACT at The Windybrow Theatre in Johannesburg, directed by Sandra Kotze.

My thanks to Denys Webb for a magical first production. I also particularly wish to remember Mark Howarth who created an unforgettable Tommie and died so tragically young.

Set

Time Some time during the first half of the 20th Century.

Place A simple house in a small country town.

Setting The living room and Ma's bedroom. The entire area is covered by a cracked and well-worn linoleum. Vestiges of the original pattern – green leaves and red roses – can still be discerned. The back wall of the living room is transparent. When the living room is dimly lit a deep midnight blue sky and the suggestion of fruit trees in blossom can be glimpsed through the transparent scrim. The living room takes up three quarters of the stage space. Ma's room is divided from the living room by the section of a wall and a door. The living room is a fairly big but rather empty room. Right centre there is a heavy dining room table with chairs on either side. Above the table a heavy lamp casts a stark light. This is the only light in the room which melts away into the gloomy corners. The kitchen door is back left. The passage door is front left. Ma's bedroom door is back right. In the transparent back wall, to the left, is an outside door. The wooden door is open but a gauze outer door is closed. To the right of this door there is a tall, dark and ominous looking cupboard with a single door and a key in the lock. Right back, next to the wall dividing Ma's bedroom from the living room, is a dark wooden chest. Ma's bedroom is slightly recessed so that there can be a window in the short left wall. This part of the wall is at a sharp diagonal and the window is open. Under the window is a small bench. Ma's narrow bed stands in the corner against the back wall and the wall on the right. Next to the bed is a small table. On the table are glasses and an oil lamp. Right front, against the wall, is a chest of drawers.

Lights The set is dimly lit and atmospheric. Both rooms remain lit throughout the play. However, the lights grow bright and dim to focus the action in a particular area.

Sound From time to time there is the sound of crickets chirping in the back yard.

Scene 1

Lights up on MA's room and, very dimly, on the living room.

MA: (*Calling loudly.*) Tommie! Tommie!!
(*TOMMIE enters from the kitchen. Runs across the living room and appears breathless in the doorway of MA's room. He is wearing a frilly apron.*)
Just look at you Tommie! Take that off at once!

TOMMIE: I'm helping with the tart. Sophie says my hands are strong and she has rheumatism.

MA: Always doing something for Sophie. Always at her beck and call. From morn to night. You never get any fresh air. Is that a life for a young man, I ask you?
(*SOPHIE enters from kitchen. She is carrying an ironing blanket over her one arm. Lights come up on the living room.*)

SOPHIE: (*Mutters.*) Baby's birthday cake has fallen flat. (*Shakes out blanket and throws it over the table.*)

TOMMIE: (*Frightened.*) It's Sophie!

SOPHIE: (*Calling.*) Tommie! Where have you got to! You have work to do!

TOMMIE: (*Calling from MA's room.*) Ma wants water!

SOPHIE: Hurry up then! The tart can't wait!
(*TOMMIE leaves MA's room, runs across the living room and goes into the kitchen.*)

TOMMIE: (*From kitchen.*) Baby is almost here! It's getting dark! (*Enters living room.*) Yes! Baby is almost here!

MA: (*In her room.*) My Baby. My little girl. My lovely little Baby...

TOMMIE: (*Enters MA's room with the glass of water.*) Here I am Ma.

MA: Thank you.

SOPHIE: (*In living room. Muttering.*) Always wanting something. It never stops. Never a moment's peace.

TOMMIE: Is that all Ma? I must go. Sophie is waiting.

MA: Tommie, my boy...

TOMMIE: Yes Ma?

MA: Please bring the water in the flowered cup. You know the one. It's a very special day today.

81

TOMMIE: Yes Ma. I forgot. (*Runs out of the room. Crosses the living room.*)

MA: And be careful! Don't break it!

TOMMIE: I won't Ma! (*Exits to the kitchen.*)

SOPHIE: Well at least she didn't keep you with one of her stories! Stoke the coals! I need a hot oven!

TOMMIE: (*Enters from kitchen with a cup of water.*) Ma wants water. (*Walks quickly to MA's room.*)

SOPHIE: Not again! Well be quick about it!

MA: (*In her room.*) First they were twelve...and as the years passed...they broke...and now there's only one...only one left. (*She reaches out and puts on her glasses.*)
(*TOMMIE appears with the cup.*)
Thank you Tommie. (*Takes the cup.*)
(*TOMMIE turns to exit.*)
Sit there my child.

TOMMIE: But...

MA: Sit down.
(*TOMMIE sits down.*)
Do you see this cup?

SOPHIE: (*In the living room.*) There it starts again. The psalm about the cup.
(*As MA continues to speak about the cup SOPHIE mouths the words with her.*)

MA: First there were twelve. First there were twelve. And then they all broke. And now there is only one. Just look. See how pretty it is.
(*SOPHIE exits to the kitchen.*)

TOMMIE: Yes Ma.

MA: Roses and violets. And look inside. You see? A small red rose right at the bottom.

TOMMIE: I see Ma.
(*From the kitchen, the sound of coal being poured into the stove. MINNIE appears in the passage and moves towards MA's room. The lights dim in the living room.*)

MA: It was a wedding gift. We got many things but the cups were the nicest. And I still remember, I took them out of the straw so carefully and put them all in a row. I called your father and said, 'Come and look. Like a garden.' But when he stood in the door he had his top hat under his arm. He said he was going to a funeral and he didn't have time. But I couldn't stop looking at them. All in a row. And...shining.

MINNIE: (*Appearing in the door.*) Good evening Ma.

MA: Evening Minnie.

MINNIE: And how do you feel Ma?

MA: Not so good Minnie.

MINNIE: I'm also not feeling very well. It's the first heat.

MA: Poor Minnie. Spring has never agreed with you. Don't you feel a little better after the rain?

MINNIE: I...don't think so.

MA: I can feel a breeze coming through the window. It smells of wet leaves. Can you smell it Tommie?

TOMMIE: (*Sniffs.*) And blossoms.

(*TOMMIE moves to the window and looks out.*)

Baby is somewhere out there. And...she's getting closer.

MINNIE: I'm just going out for a little while Ma.

MA: And where are you going Minnie?

MINNIE: To get some fresh air. It's so...stifling...in here. Well...I must be going now Ma.

MA: Wait a minute Minnie. There is something I want to say to you.

MINNIE: (*Anxiously.*) What is it Ma?

MA: Baby is coming and you mustn't say anything to make her unhappy. Do you hear me?

MINNIE: I wouldn't say anything Ma.

MA: Sometimes you can be a little unkind.

MINNIE: It's not me. It's Sophie.

MA: I won't have it Minnie. Do you hear me?

MINNIE: (*Sullenly.*) Yes Ma. Well...I suppose I should be going. (*She doesn't go.*)

MA: Look outside Tommie and tell me if you can see the moon.

TOMMIE: I can see it Ma.

MA: Where is it?

TOMMIE: It's quite high. Between the outhouse and the peach tree.

MA: And is it big?

TOMMIE: It's yellow and round. Like a sugar biscuit.

(*MINNIE turns slowly and dejectedly. She exits towards the living room. MA takes off her glasses and puts them on the table next to the bed.*)

MA: I feel a little tired now Tommie. Turn down the lamp won't you? I think I'll have a little sleep. And stay with me until I'm asleep. I feel so…funny tonight.

(*TOMMIE turns down the lamp. The lights become very dim. Then he sits down near MA and waits for her to fall asleep. Lights up in the living room.*

SOPHIE appears in the kitchen door and notices MINNIE who is sneaking quietly through the living room towards the front door.)

SOPHIE: Minnie! And where you do you think you're going?

MINNIE: (*Nervously.*) I'm just…getting some air.

SOPHIE: Do you want everyone to see you? They're all on their way to the evening service and you getting fresh air like a heathen.

MINNIE: They won't see me, Sophie. I'm going out.

SOPHIE: (*Outraged.*) Out?

(*MINNIE squeaks.*)

And where are you going?

TOMMIE: (*Entering from the bedroom.*) Here I am Sophie!

SOPHIE: Go to your bedroom Tommie!

TOMMIE: But the tart…

SOPHIE: I'll do that myself! I must talk to Minnie and it's not for your ears. Why are you just standing there! Go to your room! Polish your shoes or something! I'll call you when I need you. Go!

(*TOMMIE exits to the passage.*)

Come now Minnie. Tell me…where are you going?

MINNIE: I'm just going to see Hannah Vlok. Where else would I go? (*Tearful.*)

SOPHIE: But why now? At this time of the evening?

MINNIE: She said…that she wants to talk to me about something.

SOPHIE: And what could that be?

MINNIE: It's about…it's about…

SOPHIE: And don't lurk in the shadows. Stand where I can see you. Now speak clearly. What are you hiding from me?

MINNIE: It's about…the curse. It came…and now it won't stop. For days and days. The doctors want to cut. They say…her womb has dropped.

SOPHIE: And why does she want to talk to you about such things?

MINNIE: She knows…that I've been under the knife.

SOPHIE: I hope you haven't said anything!

MINNIE: About what?

SOPHIE: About…your insides.

MINNIE: I haven't said anything Sophie.

SOPHIE: Well thank goodness for that! I remember when you came out of hospital…we'd only been here for half an hour…when Hannah Vlok came over in her slippers…to see the wound. The wound! I ask you! I told her quite plainly a wound…is a private matter…

MINNIE: Yes…Sophie…

SOPHIE: That Hannah has no sense of decency. No background. You can tell that. In such poor taste. Speaking openly…about such things. About private parts and insides. Such things are kept only to your immediate family. And then only if you have to.

MINNIE: Yes Sophie. I understand. Can I go now?

SOPHIE: Most certainly not! I said I wanted to speak to you! (*Heavy tolling of a church bell. The bells strikes seven.*)

MINNIE: (*Closing her ears.*) Oh the bell! (*Tearful.*) That bell! The endless bell! Night and day! It gives me a headache!

SOPHIE: Forget about the bell Minnie. Do you know what day it is?

MINNIE: (*Tearful.*) Yes…it's…Sunday.

SOPHIE: Of course it's Sunday! But do you know what day it is?
(*MINNIE squeaks.*)
I'll tell you what day it is. It's the sixteenth of September. Look at me when I speak to you!

MINNIE: (*Presses her handkerchief over her mouth.*) Yes, Sophie.

SOPHIE: And on the sixteenth of September it is Baby's birthday!

MINNIE: I…just forgot.

SOPHIE: You forgot?

(*SOPHIE exits to the kitchen.*)

MINNIE: (*Calling after her.*) It's because I don't feel well!
These days I don't feel well at all!

SOPHIE: (*From the kitchen.*) And what happens on Baby's
birthday? Each year? For twelve years?

MINNIE: (*Pathetic.*) She comes…to visit us.

SOPHIE: (*Enters with a bowl filled with water. Triumphantly.*)
Yes! That's right! She comes to visit us! Once a year she
comes to visit us for just one hour. You know that very
well. And that is why you've chosen to go out tonight. How
can you do that? It's because you want to leave me alone
with her! Because Ma is sick you want to run away like the
coward you are!

MINNIE: It's not that. It's just…

SOPHIE: Spit it out!

MINNIE: It's because…I don't want to see her again!

SOPHIE: And why not!

(*The distant sound of a hymn being sung in the church. It is a
melancholy hymn and the congregation sing listlessly, drawing
out the vowels. After each verse there is a light pause and then
the hymn continues as before. The singing can be heard until
otherwise indicated in the text.*)

MINNIE: It's just…it's just…that she…makes me feel so old.
Every year we get older…and uglier…you and I. But not
she…she stays just as pretty… Nothing is ever changed…
She was always the prettiest…

SOPHIE: How can you speak like that! Envy is a deadly sin!

MINNIE: Pretty Baby…my little doll…she was always our
father's favourite.

SOPHIE: (*Agonized.*) That's not true. That's not true!

MINNIE: (*Tearful.*) Yes it is! We never sat on his lap…rode on
his foot…and you know it!

SOPHIE: Because she was always wheedling and begging!
Wicked…even then!

MINNIE: But it's not being old and ugly… It's to be old…so
alone… Look at me…Minnie Roos…thirty-six …without
ovaries and on the shelf! And it's her fault! There were

young men who visited me on Sunday afternoons. There
was Hennie Haarhof from Red Hills.

SOPHIE: (*Disdainfully.*) Hendrick Haarhof!

MINNIE: And Dirkie Venter.

SOPHIE: (*Even more disdainfully.*) Dirkie Venter!

MINNIE: Someone would have asked me! I know it! I could
have been married. I could have had a husband. A life
companion. Yes… I could have! If it hadn't been for her!
Then I became unholy! Baby Roos's sister! And no one
wanted anything to do with me!

SOPHIE: It's true. She brought shame on our family.

MINNIE: And from then on I have been trapped in this dark
house between the church and the mortuary! And why
must it always be like this? Windows closed. Curtains.
Shutters!

SOPHIE: Do you want the people to peer at us? Do you want
to be like Ma? Everything wide open! Without shame!

MINNIE: If only I could get out of here! But where would I
go? Only to Hannah Vlok who speaks about puff pastry
and insides! Because everywhere there are townspeople
who whisper behind their hands and who look at us over
their shoulders. And it's because of her! And that is why
I don't want to be here when she comes…because every
time I see her I have to bottle it up and I can't any more!
(*She starts crying and presses her handkerchief against her eyes.*)

SOPHIE: And what about me! What about me? I also have to
live in the shadow of her sin! Do you think it's easy? (*Moves
towards the chest and opens it.*) But you always feel so sorry
for yourself. Minnie…Minnie…Minnie! It's always about
you.
(*Takes a white tablecloth out of the kist. Closes the kist with a
heavy thud. Moves to the table again. Shakes out the tablecloth
and opens it on the table. As she continues to speak she sprinkles
water on the tablecloth in order to iron it. She does this until
otherwise indicated in the text.*
A short silence. MINNIE wrings her hands.)

MINNIE: Please Sophie… I want to go out now… I can't stay
here another minute… I can't bear it. (*Starts crying.*)

SOPHIE: Stop that! I told you I want to speak to you. You're not leaving this house. You're not putting your foot out of this house and that is a fact. (*Sits down.*) And be quiet. What I have to tell you is very, very important. Don't just stand there. Sit. I'm telling you to sit!

(*MINNIE goes slowly to the chair and sits. She looks despondent and tearful.*)

Minnie...prepare yourself for the worst.

MINNIE: (*Frightened.*) What is it?

SOPHIE: I don't really want to tell you. I don't want to give you...palpitations again. I would do it alone if I could. But I should take care of myself. I'm also not strong you know. Even though you're the delicate one. With your operation and your fainting fits and your endless headaches. The truth is...you'll outlive me by years. No, I won't make old bones. That's what you think. You don't know what I suffer...in my cold room. On my narrow bed. You don't know! But this isn't the time. We have to stand together, Minnie. We must give each other strength.

(*MINNIE sniffles.*)

Stop that.

(*MINNIE wipes her eyes.*)

The truth is, Minnie...something isn't right. I've known for a long time. Suspected...something. I spoke to Ma about it but she didn't want to hear. Baby has always been her pet. Like Tommie. That's because they take after her side of the family. I don't want to say things about our father but sometimes I don't know how he could have married that woman. This time I'm not going to lock myself in my room when she comes.

MINNIE: (*Amazed.*) You're not?

SOPHIE: No, I'm not. I have my duty to the family. With Ma...out of the way...I can do what has to be done. At last. No one will stop me this time.

MINNIE: What are you going to do Sophie?

SOPHIE: And you are going to help me.

MINNIE: I...don't feel very well today. Seeing Baby always makes me feel ill. And for weeks afterwards I'm so dizzy and I can hardly lift my head.

SOPHIE: Then you'll be glad to know that if my plan
    succeeds you will never have to see her again.

MINNIE: (*Delighted and amazed.*) You mean that she'll go away
    and never come back?

SOPHIE: That's right. Never.

MINNIE: And I never have to look at her face again…and
    her…bright eyes.

SOPHIE: You won't have to. Not ever.

MINNIE: What are you going to do? (*Eagerly.*) Are you going
    to shout at her? Point your finger and tell her what you
    think of her? Are you going to chase her out of the house?

SOPHIE: (*Shakes her head.*) It's not that easy, poor Minnie…if
    only you knew.

MINNIE: (*Suspicious.*) Knew what?

SOPHIE: I can't tell you. Oh, you'll get hysterical. And that is
    for sure. And you'll spoil everything.

MINNIE: I won't. I promise. You can slap me if I do.
    (*The singing ends.*)

SOPHIE: I'll have to take it step by step. Yes, that's the only
    way. Otherwise it will be too much of a shock. I'll get
    some water for you and you can take a powder for your
    headache.

MINNIE: But I don't have one.

SOPHIE: You will. Believe me. You have to keep calm that's
    all I ask of you. (*SOPHIE exits to the kitchen.*)
    (*MINNIE is alone on the stage. She looks nervous, wrings her
    hands and whimpers. SOPHIE returns with a glass of water
    and a headache powder and gives it to MINNIE.*)
    There.
    (*MINNIE puts the headache powder in the water.*)
    Well, where must I begin? (*Suddenly tearful.*) It's at times
    like these that I miss our dear father the most. I can almost
    see him coming through that door. With his top hat on
    his head. 'Everything went as planned,' he'd say. Then he
    would hang the heavy key on the hook, take off his frock
    coat and his top hat. He would give them to me. He knew
    he didn't even have to ask. I would brush them until there
    wasn't even a speck of dust.

MINNIE: Come now Sophie! I've had my powder. I'm
keeping calm. Now you can tell me.

SOPHIE: Yes…yes. (*Sitting down. Closes her eyes.*) Father would
say these things are sent to test us. (*Opens her eyes. Wipes
the corners of her mouth with her forefinger.*) Let me ask you
Minnie. Have you noticed anything…strange about Baby?

MINNIE: What do you mean?

SOPHIE: About…her dress, for instance.

MINNIE: No. (*Thinking.*) It's a nice dress. You sewed it.

SOPHIE: Anything else?

MINNIE: It's always clean and fresh. Looks like it's just been
washed.

SOPHIE: Minnie…Minnie! (*Tries to keep calm.*) Surely…you
must be…surprised that's it's always the same dress.

MINNIE: It's her confirmation dress. Her best dress. She
always wears it when she's going out.

SOPHIE: Let me put this another way. How many years has
it been since…since she ran off like that? How many? I'm
asking you Minnie!

MINNIE: Don't speak so loudly. (*Tearful. Putting her hands over
her ears.*) You're frightening me.

SOPHIE: I'm sorry. Just tell me.

MINNIE: Eight…no ten…

SOPHIE: Twelve years! She was eighteen when she left and
today she's turning thirty.

MINNIE: You're right. The time passes so quickly. And
nothing ever happens to me. Year after year. One like
the other. But not for her! Oh no! She's gone out into the
world. Seen things. Been places!

SOPHIE: Be quiet! Listen to me. The same dress. Every time.

MINNIE: I didn't really notice. Maybe…she changed it once
or twice. I don't really look at her. I can't bear to look at
her!

SOPHIE: Well, I see everything. Nothing escapes me. And
I'm telling you.

MINNIE: And how do you suddenly know everything? When
you lock yourself in your room every time?

SOPHIE: I have to go outside don't I? To the… convenience.
I'm only human after all. And whenever I crossed the

yard…I would stand at the window (*Indicates the back window.*) and look in. Only because I was concerned about you. I wanted to…to see if you were too pale and overwrought. Each time I tried not to look at her. But I couldn't help it. It's such a small room and there were only three of you. It's not only the dress that is the same. Everything. Her hair. Her face. She never changes! Never looks a day older. And how can she stay the same while we age every year? Have you ever thought of that?

MINNIE: Not really… Maybe…because she's happy. They say misery makes you old. Maybe (*Tearful.*) because she doesn't have to get up at dawn to take the slops buckets out and shovel the coal into the stove. This life…has made me old and ugly.

SOPHIE: No…it's not only that. I mean…exactly as she looked before. Is that…natural, I ask you?

MINNIE: I don't know.

SOPHIE: Think, Minnie. Think for once. And another thing…why does she never eat all the nice things we make for her? She always leaves them on her plate.

MINNIE: I don't know.

SOPHIE: And the presents? What does she do with them?

MINNIE: (*Thinks.*) She always asks Tommie to keep them for her. Until the next year.

SOPHIE: Just as I thought! (*Darkly.*) She doesn't need them where she's going.

MINNIE: Yes, yes I'm sure she has so many nice things, I'm sure she's used to better. She doesn't want our little presents. (*Sniffs.*)

SOPHIE: That's not what I mean.

MINNIE: Just look at the ring he gave her. Big, shining thing. It must have cost a fortune.

SOPHIE: It's a cheap and nasty piece of glass. Didn't cost a shilling. You don't seem to understand what I'm telling you!
(*MINNIE sulks.*)
It…took me a long time to realise. But now…I'm almost sure.

MINNIE: About what?

SOPHIE: (*Bursting out.*) About her! About her. That's not our
    Baby. Not as we used to know her.

MINNIE: It looks like Baby.

SOPHIE: I mean she *is* Baby and she *isn't.*

MINNIE: You're confusing me! I'm feeling quite dizzy. And
    my palms are sweaty.

SOPHIE: It's not our Baby, it's not Baby as we used to know
    her.

MINNIE: But you said she was the same. Now you're telling
    me she's different.

SOPHIE: She's not the Baby that she was. (*Whispers hoarsely.*)
    When she was alive!

MINNIE: Sophie! You don't mean...what are you saying?
    (*Handkerchief in front of her mouth. High-pitched whine.*)

SOPHIE: I'm sorry...I'm just saying that she might...I mean
    might...be an apparition. Mind you I'm not saying it's
    certain.
    (*MINNIE hyperventilates.*)
    All the signs are there. I've heard about such things.
    And I've asked about it. All the signs. Never changing.
    Suddenly appearing out of nowhere.

MINNIE: It's not true! You're trying to frighten me! She
    comes on the five o'clock train and she walks from the
    station.

SOPHIE: Why doesn't anyone ever see her? Why doesn't
    Hannah Vlok come over. Such a busybody. Even Elsie
    Koen. She's always sitting on her verandah.

MINNIE: I don't know. Maybe she doesn't walk along the
    road.

SOPHIE: Does she knock? Does she even ring the doorbell?
    Oh, my poor sister. I don't want to be the one to tell you.
    Really I don't. You must believe me.

MINNIE: (*Tearful.*) It's too horrible to think of. Too horrible.

SOPHIE: I can only hope that I'm wrong. But if I'm right...
    I wouldn't be surprised, let me put it like that. After what
    she did. After her shameless wickedness... how could she
    know any rest. It would be her punishment. An unquiet

spirit wandering the earth. (*Extremely bitterly.*) Even after what she did... Ma would hear no wrong. Always Baby this and Baby that.

MINNIE: Yes. It's true. And what about me? Down on my knees scrubbing the linoleum. And never a kind word.

SOPHIE: And all the little names she calls her. 'My lamb.' 'My heart.'

MINNIE: She never calls me anything! Just Minnie! Minnie, Minnie...plain...and ugly! (*Tearful.*)

SOPHIE: Yes. Just look at them. Just look at them. The one...a sinful little slut! And the other...simple-minded.

MINNIE: Don't talk like that about Tommie. You'll be punished.

SOPHIE: (*Darkly.*) I would be surprised...if there was a drop of our father's blood in her veins.

MINNIE: What do you mean?

SOPHIE: A woman...with such a reputation. A woman... like that. You know what the people used to whisper about her? But I'd better not say another word. (*Suddenly excited. Remembering.*) And they don't cry either. Never real tears! Have you ever seen her crying?

MINNIE: I...don't think so.

SOPHIE: There you are! And if they're cut, or if they're stabbed they don't bleed. Not a drop. And the shadow! They don't cast a shadow. And you can't see their reflection in a mirror! If I remember anything more I'll tell you.

MINNIE: Oh...oh... I think I'm going to faint.

SOPHIE: Don't you dare! I need you at my side. We need to keep our eyes wide open. We are entering...into the deepest peril. We don't know...what she is capable of... Such...a creature from the nether realm...

(*MINNIE gives a little shriek and runs from the room exiting to the passage. SOPHIE looks after her, shakes her head and clicks her tongue.*)

(*Calling after her.*) Lie down for a little! And calm yourself!

(*SOPHIE sighs heavily and shakes her head. She moves slowly and heavily towards the kitchen. For a moment the stage is empty, then she re-emerges from the kitchen. She is carrying an iron. It*) *is red hot. She starts ironing the tablecloth. Every time she puts down the iron, it is with a heavy thud. As SOPHIE continues to iron she mutters angrily to herself. Her voice rises and falls with the angry muttering. This continues for a minute or so. Then, without even raising her head, she calls loudly.)*

Tommie! Tommie!! (*She continues to iron.*)

(*After a few seconds TOMMIE appears in the passage door. He is still wearing his apron.*)

TOMMIE: Here I am Sophie.

SOPHIE: (*Without lifting her head.*) Get back into the kitchen. Put the dough in the dish and the dish in the oven. And don't forget the sugar-beans. To keep it from rising.

(*TOMMIE moves into the kitchen.*)

(*Calling after him.*) And what did the family choose? The marble or the granite?

TOMMIE: (*Calling from the kitchen.*) The granite!

SOPHIE: Which one?

TOMMIE: (*Off.*) Speckled!

SOPHIE: Poor Lettie. They don't seem to be spending much money on her. And have they chosen a text?

TOMMIE: (*Off.*) Yes. 'Rest in Peace'!

SOPHIE: (*Outraged.*) Nothing else?

TOMMIE: (*Off.*) No!

SOPHIE: Poor thing. Remember, Tommie…my inscription has been neatly written out! You'll find it in my top drawer with my surgical stocking! You won't forget?

TOMMIE: (*Off.*) No, Sophie!

SOPHIE: (*To herself.*) Talking about surgical stocking. I'm wearing three pairs, one on top of the other. My varicose veins are so swollen and blue. That's because I had to stand for hours in the cold cellar. My shoes getting wet from the melting ice. (*Looks down towards the cellar.*) Lettie is a big woman. I used two cakes of carbolic soap. Even if I was tired. There was nothing I forgot to do. Whenever I wash them I can feel our father watching me. Saying, 'Yes, Sophie my child. That's how I taught you.' And then… there is the viewing. (*Calling.*) When is it Tommie? When is it? The viewing?

TOMMIE: (*Off.*) I don't know!

SOPHIE: (*Calling.*) I'll have to ask Mr Vogel! When our father was alive, we knew everything. Not only about viewings and funerals, but about the sick and the dying! Even before someone breathed his last, our father was ready for him! Our father was the most respected undertaker in the whole province! And the best dressed! Such a pity that Mr Vogel has to look after our business! With his cheap hat, his frayed cuffs and his jacket that is never pressed! Our father had such high hopes for you, Tommie! That you would follow in his footsteps! And all you can be now…is a poor apprentice. That's why he put '& Son' onto his name when you were born. 'Visser & Son.' (*Very heavy sigh.*) But poor Tommie…we know it's not your fault! I know.

TOMMIE: (*Appears in the doorway.*) I'm sorry.

SOPHIE: Well, it's no use dwelling on the past. We have to make the best of things.

MA: (*Softly, calling from the bedroom.*) Help! Help me! Heeeelp!

SOPHIE: At least they gave me a good black dress for her to wear. Dark stockings. So she won't look so enormous.

MA: (*Calling louder.*) Help me! Help! Heeeelp!

SOPHIE: And a hat with pheasant feathers… That should impress them at the viewing.

TOMMIE: I think I hear…

MA: Heeeelp!

TOMMIE: It's Ma! (*He runs towards her room.*)
(*SOPHIE follows him. Lights up on MA's room and dim on the living room.*)
(*In the door of MA's room.*) What is it Ma? Ma?

SOPHIE: (*Entering and shaking MA.*) What's happened Ma? What's wrong?

MA: (*Confused.*) What is it?

SOPHIE: It's me Ma, it's Sophie and Tommie. What's wrong Ma? How do you feel Ma?

MA: (*Mutters.*) Water…give me some water…
(*SOPHIE gives MA the cup.*)
(*To SOPHIE angrily.*) Help me to sit up…do you want me to choke?

SOPHIE: (*Helps MA up and puts the cup to her lips.*) Tommie,
turn up the lamp.

(*TOMMIE turns up the lamp.*)

MA: (*To SOPHIE.*) You're hurting me. Stop fiddling with me!

SOPHIE: There you are now. Is that better? (*She lowers MA
onto the pillows.*)

MA: I had a dream. A terrible dream.

TOMMIE: What did you dream, Ma?

SOPHIE: (*Mutters.*) Is that all? I had the fright of my life. I
thought you were seeing an apparition or something.

MA: (*Seeing TOMMIE in his apron.*) Tommie, why are you still
wearing that?

TOMMIE: I'm still helping Sophie Ma. Please tell me about
the dream. I like dreams.

SOPHIE: (*Angrily.*) I can't do everything alone.

MA: It's no life for a young man.

SOPHIE: Are you feeling better Ma? We have things to do.

MA: (*Firmly.*) You can go but Tommie must stay here.

SOPHIE: But he's helping me Ma.

MA: Sophie I don't feel very good and I want him here. I
want him to sit with me.

SOPHIE: (*Sighs.*) Very well then. (*Exits muttering.*) I have to go
and decorate the cake.

MA: (*Calling after her.*) Is it a pink cake?

SOPHIE: (*In the living room.*) Yes!

MA: With many small roses?

SOPHIE: Yes!

(*MA smiles with contentment. SOPHIE continues to iron the
tablecloth.*)

TOMMIE: (*Goes to the window and looks out.*) She must be very
near. Maybe she's feeling the apricots are ripe. If they're
ripe.

MA: Yes my child. Oh I miss her so much when she's not
here. Tommie…you must look after Baby when she comes.

TOMMIE: Look after her Ma?

MA: Yes. I don't want her to be sad. You know…Minnie and
Sophie…can say such unkind things. I don't think they
mean to, but Baby has a soft heart. Like you.

TOMMIE: Yes Ma. My heart is soft.

MA: I don't want them to dwell on the past. All that is gone
and it doesn't matter any more. After all, she is happy
now. To tell you the truth my child…I'm glad she left. Yes,
I can say it now. (*Small silence. MA closes her eyes and thinks.*)
I remember it like yesterday. The sun wasn't even up. I
woke up and she was kneeling at my bed and talking very
softly. She didn't want to wake your father. She told me she
was running away with him. Your father…had forbidden
him the house you see. When she left I went to the window
and looked out. I saw her in the moonlight…running up
the garden path. She opened the gate…then she was gone.
And I thought, 'My little girl, yes my little girl. Run…run
away. Away from the thick walls…the watchful eyes…the
cold cellar with the blocks of ice.' Oh…my heart wanted
to break. But she promised to visit every year. And she's
never broken her promise, not even once. She's a good
girl. You're good children, both of you. And so…if they say
anything harsh to her…you must come and tell me.

TOMMIE: I will Ma.

MA: (*Sighs deeply.*) Oh the dream…it's as if it stays with me. So
lovely…but so frightening.

TOMMIE: What is it, Ma?

MA: It's the dream! It stays with me.

(*TOMMIE sits on the bench under the window.*)

TOMMIE: What did you dream Ma? Tell me Ma?

MA: I don't think I'll ever forget it. It's so clear.

TOMMIE: Tell me Ma. Come now Ma.

MA: Very well my child. I dreamt I was lying on the bed.
This bed. And there were people standing around the bed.
They were looking down at me. Then I felt how I started
drifting up in the air…just above the bed. And then higher
and higher till I was close to the ceiling.

TOMMIE: And then Ma?

MA: Then I looked down and I saw myself on the bed. I was
very pale and very still. Then Sophie closed my eyes and
folded my hands and told Minnie to put sheets over all the
mirrors. You were also next to the bed. Suddenly I saw that
the window was open and I thought I must go and get a

little fresh air. And I'd hardly thought that… when I was outside. And then it was as if I wasn't drifting any more…it was as if I could fly just where I wanted to. Not really fly. But not like a bird. Like…like I always swam in Uncle Theuns' farm dam. Swim-fly.

(*Silence as she seems to think back.*)

TOMMIE: How is that Ma?

MA: Like this my child. (*Illustrates.*)

TOMMIE: Tell me more Ma. About the dream.

MA: I'm a bit tired now my child. I think I must rest a while.

TOMMIE: Please Ma. Tell me. Just tell me quickly.

MA: Very well then. Where was I?

TOMMIE: (*Sits down again.*) Outside Ma.

MA: Yes…yes…that's right. Well…then I flew low over the back garden. And I could see so clearly. Even without my glasses. And then…it was as if I was hearing things I'd never heard before.

TOMMIE: What do you mean Ma?

MA: I could hear…the pear tree…budding…you know…the small buds swelling out…just like bubbles in a porridge pot. And also…the compost heap…seething and fermenting.

TOMMIE: Yes Ma?

MA: And the chickens' little hearts ticking like small pocket watches. And there I saw Aunt Hannah where she was busy pulling weeds from the radish bed…and as she moved her head this way and that way I could hear the wax moving in her ears.

TOMMIE: And then Ma? And then?

MA: Then I was flying over Aunt Hannah's ranunculus… you can't imagine what ranunculus sound like!… When a very big hand came out of the clouds…a big hand with long, white fingers…

TOMMIE: Ma!

MA: And the hand came closer…and closer as if it wanted to catch me. I went to sit in the branches of the pear tree and I tried to hide between the blossoms. And then I heard a big voice saying, 'Why are you wasting time Magdalena Susarah Roos? What on earth are you doing there? Time to go to heaven!' And then I saw how the thin, pale fingers were curled around the tree and tried to pull it out by the roots.

TOMMIE: And then Ma?

MA: And I thought it's not so easy! I slipped through a small space between the thumb and the forefinger and I flew away. Behind me I could feel how the long fingers were stretching and grabbing but they couldn't catch me.

TOMMIE: (*Terrified.*) And then Ma? And then?

MA: And then I woke up.

TOMMIE: Oh but it's a scary dream Ma.

MA: They say if one dreams something like that...then your time is not far. I have to make my peace. You must promise me one thing my child.

TOMMIE: Yes Ma.

MA: If I pass away, you must choose a coffin for me. You work there and you know about these things. Sophie and Minnie will try and skimp and save but I want a nice dark coffin with shiny handles.

TOMMIE: I don't want you to die, Ma. You'll leave me all alone!

MA: I'll always be with you. Watching over you.

TOMMIE: Always?

MA: Yes. I promise.

(*TOMMIE seems satisfied. He goes to the window and looks out.*)

And another thing my child, I want to be buried in my wedding dress. It's in the trunk under the bed...a lovely dress... (*Thinking back.*) It's too big for me now...because now I'm so thin and gaunt...but then I was a plump young girl and as pretty as a picture.

TOMMIE: (*Looking out.*) Maybe she's in the back yard by now. Under the vine.

MA: The young men called me little partridge partridge. Because I was so sweet and plump. (*Little sigh.*) But that... was before I met your father.

TOMMIE: Maybe...she's looking at all the blossoms.

MA: He was a good man, your father. Tall and pale…with a soft voice…and sensitive fingers. (*Pause.*) But he never laughed. Never.

TOMMIE: Maybe…she's smelling the violets…or looking at the irises next to the outhouse.

MA: Sophie can make the dress smaller…she's good at doing alterations. Or maybe she can use pins. Who's going to see. But only down the back. Because old Mysie Cillier has eyes like a hawk. And she goes to every viewing, come hell or high water. No…I think Sophie must rather stitch it just to be sure. (*Pause.*) I'm very tired now. I think I must sleep for a little while. Do you hear me my child…I want to sleep for a while.

TOMMIE: Yes Ma.

MA: And something else my child…

TOMMIE: Yes Ma.

MA: Don't lay out tea and cake for the mourners. It's really so unnecessary…

TOMMIE: Yes Ma.

MA: And don't forget about the wedding dress.

TOMMIE: I won't Ma. (*Moves to the door.*)

MA: And Tommie…

TOMMIE: (*Turning back.*) Yes Ma?

MA: It will make me so happy to see her again… My girl… with her lovely shining eyes.

TOMMIE: Yes. (*Pause.*) Good night Ma. (*Goes to the door.*)

MA: Good night Tommie. Tommie…

TOMMIE: (*At the door.*) Yes Ma?

MA: Just look at the stars. How big they are. And so close. Tommie…

TOMMIE: Yes Ma?

MA: You're a good child.

TOMMIE: Thank you Ma.

(*TOMMIE exits. The lights in MA's room grow dim. TOMMIE crosses the living room. He goes to the outside door and peers out. After a moment he exits quickly to the passage.*)

Scene 2

The stage is empty. MA's room is very dimly lit. The church bell strikes one for a quarter to eight. Then the congregation can be heard singing a slow, sad psalm. The singing continues until otherwise indicated in the text. SOPHIE appears in the kitchen door. She is wearing an apron.

SOPHIE: (*Calling towards the bedrooms.*) Minnie! Come now Minnie! We have a lot to do! Minnie!! (*Mutters to herself as she tucks a lanky strand of hair back in her bun.*)
(*MINNIE appears in the bedroom door. She looks dishevelled and her eyes are swollen.*)
Minnie, you must help me to put everything on the table.

MINNIE: (*Looking at the table.*) Yes Sophie.
(*SOPHIE exits to the kitchen. MINNIE approaches the table. She strokes the tablecloth tenderly.*)

SOPHIE: (*From the kitchen.*) Minnie! Where are you!
(*MINNIE starts crying softly. She covers her face with her hands. SOPHIE enters from the kitchen. She is carrying plates and glasses.*)
And what is wrong now?

MINNIE: Nothing... (*Sniffs.*)

SOPHIE: (*Putting the plates and glasses on the table.*) Don't tell me that Minnie. I can see that something's wrong. Are you feeling unwell?

MINNIE: I'm a little dizzy...

SOPHIE: I suppose it's the shock. I can understand that. Suddenly finding out... (*Harsh whisper.*) ...that your youngest sister is almost certainly a spectre...from the nether world.

MINNIE: It's not just that... I can't help thinking...about the tablecloth...and all my other trousseau linen... yellowing and forgotten in the chest.

SOPHIE: Don't think about that Minnie.

MINNIE: All the beautiful sheets...the best linen all sewn by hand.

SOPHIE: I've told you to make peace with that.

MINNIE: And all my night-dresses with the many tucks.

SOPHIE: Forget about it Minnie. And know that our sister
has been punished for what she did to us. Cast into…outer
darkness.

MINNIE: I could have been a bride…with an organ playing
and a church filled with flowers.

SOPHIE: Minnie if I told you once I've told you many times
– forget about it! Come and help me. (*Exits to the kitchen.*)
(*MINNIE follows SOPHIE to the kitchen.*)
(*From within the kitchen.*) You take the ginger beer and the
tart and I'll carry the birthday cake.
(*After a few seconds SOPHIE enters from the kitchen followed by
MINNIE. They carry the items as described by SOPHIE.*)
The birthday cake didn't rise so well. But I put in a nice
jam filling. (*She puts the birthday cake on the table.*)

MINNIE: (*Putting the ginger beer and the tarts on the table.*) It's
just…sometimes when I go to bed…and I've blown out
the candle…I wonder what it would be like…to have a
husband next to me.

SOPHIE: (*Shocked.*) Minnie!

MINNIE: What it would be like…for him to hold my arm…
when we walk to the river…as the sun sets.

SOPHIE: Minnie…I didn't know you had these thoughts.
Listen to me Minnie… And do what I tell you. When you
go to sleep you must sleep on your back. You must pull
the sheets and blankets up to expose your feet. Even when
it's very cold. That will keep you…from having unholy
thoughts. (*Strokes MINNIE's arm.*) Never mind it's not so
bad. It's not so bad. Go and fetch the birthday candles and
then you can come and put them on the cake.

MINNIE: Yes Sophie. Where are they?

SOPHIE: Don't you know by this time? In the napkin drawer.
(*Sighs.*) At least I'm not tormented by such thoughts.
(*The singing stops. MINNIE goes towards the kitchen and exits.
SOPHIE speaks loudly so that MINNIE can hear.*)
No…I think only of high and elevated things! That is
because I take after the Roos family! Virtuous people! Pale
and neat!
(*MINNIE enters from the kitchen with the birthday candles.*)
Now put the candles in the cake and be quick about it.

MINNIE: (*As she continues to speak she pushes the candles into the cake. Each movement testifies of her frustration and her anger.*) One two three four five eight ten…eleven twelve! For twelve years I have been trapped in this airless house. For twelve years! I can't breathe any more…It smells of bedpans…and carbolic soap…and embalming fluid.

SOPHIE: Come now Minnie. Stop it! I'm sick and tired! (*MINNIE storms down the passage towards the passage door.*) And where're you going Minnie?

MINNIE: I have to get out of here! I must get air! I feel as if I'm suffocating! (*MINNIE can be heard opening the front door.*)

SOPHIE: Come back Minnie! At once! Or you'll be sorry! (*Short silence.*) I'm warning you! (*Short silence.*) And close the door! (*Short silence and then the front door is closed. MINNIE appears and she stands in the passage door.*) And what will they think? Storming out of here like a wild animal. And everyone coming out of church!

MINNIE: No one will even look at me. I'm just Minnie… Minnie. No one is interested in me. (*She cries.*)

SOPHIE: Oh not again!

MINNIE: (*Presses her handkerchief against her mouth.*) I saw them…coming out of the church…two by two…and here I am…so all…alone.

SOPHIE: You must stop it Minnie! You must stop feeling sorry for yourself! You must count your blessings! You don't have ovaries that's true…and you also don't have a husband…but there are others who have had to endure far worse. Just think of our dear departed father. Our poor father. You know what Hannah Vlok told us about Ma before her wedding? (*Whispers hoarsely.*) How she was seen in the company of some fly-by-night. With a large moustache and silk hat. (*Seeing the candles.*) Oh no! Why so deep! (*Fiddles with the candles as she continues to speak.*) They say he arrived out of the blue and he vanished without a trace. A smoker and a drinker and a gambler. Yes…she told us that everyone knew…expect our poor departed father. Our poor father. He was too unworldly to know about that. Just think Minnie…to lose your dear beloved wife…then to choose another life partner…only to find… on your wedding night…that things were not… as they should be. (*Darkly. Quoting.*) Remember Minnie, 'A fallen woman…is like a dark, deep pit…and the unsuspecting fools…will fall right in it.' (*Still fiddling with the candles.*) And so skew! (*Goes to MINNIE and pats her on the shoulders.*) There you are. Forget about your sorrows and think about the glory that awaits all the humble and the virtuous. And don't forget…this night we will be released from our terrible afflictions. (*Looking at the cake.*) I suppose that will have to do.

(*TOMMIE appears in the passage door.*)

TOMMIE: I'm dressed. I'm ready.

(*TOMMIE is neatly dressed in a suit which is a little too small for him. His hair is slicked down and neatly parted in the middle.*)

SOPHIE: That's right Tommie. Just in time.

TOMMIE: (*Looking at MINNIE.*) And what's wrong with her?

SOPHIE: Oh nothing…it's just the heat.

MINNIE: I think…I think… (*She presses her handkerchief in front of her mouth.*)

SOPHIE: My poor sister…why don't you go and loosen your stays? Tommie will help me with the rest.

(*MINNIE exits hastily.*)

Tommie, go and fetch the little bench in the kitchen.

(*TOMMIE exits hastily towards the kitchen.*)

(*Calls to TOMMIE in the kitchen.*) There is something I want to ask you Tommie.

(*TOMMIE re-emerges carrying the bench. He moves to the table and puts the bench down.*)

I saw you speaking to Ben earlier today. What were you saying to him?

TOMMIE: I can't remember Sophie.

SOPHIE: You mustn't speak to the Vloks. They are not our class of people.

TOMMIE: Yes Sophie.

SOPHIE: I hope you didn't tell him about Baby coming to visit us. You must never mention Baby's name again. It's no one's business but our own.

TOMMIE: You've told me. Many times.

SOPHIE: That's right.

TOMMIE: But I don't understand.

SOPHIE: My poor Tommie…you don't understand much, do you?

TOMMIE: The other people get visits from their family. They don't have to keep it a secret.

SOPHIE: This is different.

TOMMIE: How?

SOPHIE: Mercifully…you don't understand very much. And that is how it should be. Let me just say that Baby did something very wrong. Wrong and wicked. And no one wants to be reminded of it. It will only start their tongues wagging again. Do you remember when we had to keep off the streets? When no one would greet us? Or even sit in the same pew? When they cut us dead.

TOMMIE: But…

SOPHIE: No buts! You must keep your mouth shut and that's that. Then I'm not going to say another word.

TOMMIE: Yes Sophie.

(*MINNIE appears in the passage door. She is breathless and looks flustered.*)

MINNIE: I've just looked at the clock! Sophie it's almost time! What are we going to do?

SOPHIE: Get ready. And that's all. She mustn't notice…anything out of the ordinary. That above all. Everything as it used to be.

MINNIE: Yes Sophie. But we must be quick!

(*Pace intensifies.*)

TOMMIE: (*Looking out of the window.*) Maybe…she can see me here at the window.

SOPHIE: Come away there Tommie. Why are you standing there and peering out into the night? I told you we had a lot of things to do. The lamp has been smoking. Get on the table and turn the wick down.

TOMMIE: I don't want to. I'm wearing my Sunday clothes.
Why can't Minnie?

SOPHIE: Minnie! Do you want her wound to start
suppurating again?

(*MINNIE squeaks. TOMMIE moves unwillingly to the table
and while SOPHIE and MINNIE continue to talk he gets on
the table and turns down the wick.*)

(*To MINNIE.*) And where are the embroidered
handkerchiefs? They're not here. We must put them on the
table. Get them Minnie and be quick!

MINNIE: (*Nervously.*) But where are they Sophie?

SOPHIE: Don't you know anything! In the sewing box in my
cupboard.

(*MINNIE exits rapidly.*)

Tommie! You nearly stood on the tart! And be careful of
the cake! There are only three glasses. (*Calling to MINNIE.*)
There are only three glasses Minnie! Can't you do
anything properly!

(*MINNIE enters with two small white handkerchiefs. SOPHIE
moves towards the kitchen and exits as she speaks.*)

Remember Minnie. 'The all-seeing eye' comes on top with
'never sleeps' at the bottom. (*Enters with a glass in her hand
and puts it on the table.*) Tommie! Aren't you finished yet?
Oh Minnie…we don't have any matches for the birthday
candles. Go and find them!

MINNIE: Where are they?

SOPHIE: Don't you know anything? In the tin against the
wall above the stove!

(*MINNIE exits rapidly. TOMMIE climbs off the table and puts
on his shoes.*)

Be quick! The clock will strike at any moment! (*She sits at
the table.*)

(*TOMMIE sits at the table on the small bench. MINNIE enters
rapidly, puts the matches on the table and sits down.*)

And look at me! I'm still wearing my apron. What will she
think of me? Why didn't you say anything? (*Gets up. Exits
rapidly and enters almost immediately. She sits down.*)

(*The clock starts striking.*)

MINNIE: Just in time.

TOMMIE: (*Excited.*) She must be standing in the garden!

SOPHIE: Be quiet. (*SOPHIE leans across to MINNIE and starts whispering hissingly in her ear.*)
(*When the whispering stops, SOPHIE looks intently at the front door opening while MINNIE cranes her neck to look at the door leading to the back yard. Suddenly a gust of wind rustles the trees. Almost immediately BABY appears, unexpectedly, in the kitchen door.*)

TOMMIE: Baby! (*He jumps up.*)

SOPHIE: Sit! Don't you have any manners Tommie! You're at the table. Well...Baby...we're certainly glad that you're here. Aren't we Minnie?

MINNIE: Yes.

SOPHIE: Strange. I didn't hear the back door opening. (*Glances meaningfully at MINNIE.*) I'm sure I closed it earlier.
(*BABY doesn't react to this.*)
Oh well...maybe I'm wrong. As you can see...I'm not indisposed this evening. So at least I can see you this time. We are very glad to have you with us, isn't that true Minnie?

MINNIE: Yes.

BABY: (*Entering and looking at everything.*) Everything looks the same...
(*Short silence as BABY looks around.*)

SOPHIE: I was saying to Minnie just the other day, isn't that true Minnie?...that we see far too little of you. And when you do arrive...you stay for such a short time. We would like you to stay a little longer this evening. Isn't that so Minnie? (*Makes a face at MINNIE.*)

MINNIE: (*Quickly.*) Yes.

SOPHIE: Maybe an hour or two. Or possibly...you could leave tomorrow morning. It would be so nice...to see you by *daylight* for a change. (*Glances at MINNIE meaningfully.*)

BABY: I'm sorry...but I can't.

SOPHIE: And why not?

BABY: It's just...that I'm very busy. My time, you see...is not my own. (*BABY exits and goes into the kitchen.*)

TOMMIE: (*Excitedly. Calling after BABY.*) I'm lighting the candles on your cake Baby! Come and see! I'll blow them out for you as I always do!

SOPHIE: (*Sharply.*) Not this time Tommie. (*Meaningful to MINNIE. Whispering loudly.*) I want to see if she's used up her last breath or if she still has anything left.

TOMMIE: But I always do!

SOPHIE: Listen to me!

(*BABY appears in the doorway.*)

TOMMIE: Let's blow out your candles together!

(*BABY runs to the table and stands next to TOMMIE.*)

SOPHIE: No! Blow Baby. We want to see.

BABY: (*Looks mischievously at TOMMIE. Quickly and quietly.*) One, two, three.

(*BABY and TOMMIE lean forward and blow out the candles on the cake.*)

SOPHIE: Tommie! I very deliberately asked you not to! When you disobey me I get very angry!

BABY: Don't be angry with him. It's me.

TOMMIE: And look at the presents. One from me and one from Ma. I made you a flute. I carved it from a hollow reed.

BABY: (*Glad.*) I like flutes.

TOMMIE: I'll show you how to play. And this is from Ma. (*Gives her a small package.*)

BABY: (*Opening the packet.*) It's a ribbon!

TOMMIE: Such a nice colour. Why don't you put it in your hair?

BABY: I will…later. But where's Ma? Why isn't she here?

SOPHIE: I'm afraid…Ma…she is indisposed. She won't be able to see you. But don't be alarmed…it's only a temporary set-back. You know how it is…with old people?

BABY: I want to see Ma. I want to. (*Goes towards MA's room.*)

SOPHIE: You mustn't wake her. I forbid it!

(*BABY doesn't listen and continues to go towards MA's room.*)

(*Warningly.*) Baby! I'm warning you! You can't just come in here and do as you like! I won't put up with it do you hear!

(*As BABY reaches MA's door and stands in the doorway, the lights in the living room dim very slightly. The lights in MA's room grow gently brighter. While MA and BABY talk to each other, SOPHIE can be heard continuously, speaking softly and hissingly into MINNIE's ear.)*

BABY: (*Softly.*) Ma…Ma …

(*MA moans softly.*)

Ma…can you hear me?

(*MA opens her eyes and looks at BABY.*)

MA: (*Faintly.*) Is that you…my Baby?

(*BABY goes further into the room and stands near MA's bed.*)

Come and sit right next to me.

(*BABY sits on the small chair next to the bed.*)

Now let me look at you. You're as pretty as ever. Just as pretty. To see you…makes my heart glad.

BABY: It makes my heart glad too.

MA: You're a good child. And don't let anyone tell you otherwise.

BABY: No Ma.

MA: I feel so weak… I wanted to get out of bed. To put on my blue dress and wait for you as I used to. But I couldn't… The truth is…my child…I think I'm ready. And I don't want you to be sad. It's just…this poor…old body…feels much too heavy. Do you know what I mean, my child?

BABY: I do Ma. I know.

MA: You understand me, my child. Better than anyone else. (*Reaches up and touches her cheek.*) You're a child…after my own heart.

BABY: Thank you Ma.

SOPHIE: (*Calling off.*) Come now Baby! We want you to look at our presents!

MA: (*Smiling.*) They're calling you. Go now and enjoy yourself. I think I'll sleep a little …

BABY: (*Getting up.*) Yes Ma… (*Looks at MA for a few seconds and then exits.*)

(*The light in MA's room grows dim again while the lights in the living room grow brighter. BABY enters the living room. She moves to the outside door and looks out.*)

SOPHIE: Come on now Baby. Come and sit down.

BABY: (*Dreamily.*) The irises are out. So many of them.

SOPHIE: We've gone to a lot of trouble...

BABY: And the pear tree has grown. It was (*Illustrates.*) that size last time and now...it's like this.

SOPHIE: The rheumatism in my hand is bad again.

BABY: And covered in blossoms!

TOMMIE: That's because I've dug in so much horse manure.

SOPHIE: From beating the egg-whites and the cream. Come now, you have to eat something. Sit down! Stop dreaming! (*BABY returns to the table and sits down.*)
(*Ingratiatingly.*) Look, Minnie embroidered these nice handkerchiefs for you. The best linen. It's from both of us. Read the first one. There you are. (*Gives one handkerchief to BABY.*)

BABY: (*Reading.*) 'The all-seeing eye...'

SOPHIE: And now the other one. (*Passes her the handkerchief.*)

BABY: (*Reading.*) 'Never closes.'

SOPHIE: Well, aren't you going to say thank you?

BABY: Thank you.

SOPHIE: I'm sure...that will give you something to think about. Now have some birthday cake. (*Passes BABY a plate with a large slice of birthday cake on it.*)

BABY: It...looks very nice.

SOPHIE: So, why aren't you eating? Is anything wrong? (*Looks meaningfully at MINNIE.*) You won't know what it's like until you taste it. Isn't that so Minnie?

MINNIE: (*Squeaks.*) Yes.

SOPHIE: Come on now Baby, just take a bite. I slaved over a hot stove to make that.

BABY: Maybe...a little later.

SOPHIE: Just a bite. To please me. It won't kill you, will it? Don't you agree, Minnie?

MINNIE: (*Squeaks.*) Yes.

SOPHIE: Come on! To show...a little gratitude. A little... appreciation.

TOMMIE: She doesn't want to.

SOPHIE: Come now, I'm waiting. I'm getting really very angry. I'm warning you. I'll push that cake down your

throat if I have to! By heaven I will! And Minnie will help
me! Won't you Minnie?
(*MINNIE gives a smothered sob, presses her hand in front of her
mouth and rushes out towards the bedroom.*)
(*Rising.*) Minnie! Come here at once!! Minnie! (*SOPHIE
moves towards the bedroom exit.*) You'll spoil everything!
(*Exits. Off.*) Minnie!

TOMMIE: I'm sorry Baby. They're also horrible to me. Every
day. I want to go away from here. Please take me with you.
I want to go with you.

BABY: I'm sorry Tommie. I can't.

TOMMIE: But you always say that. If you don't want me to
go with you, then I'll run away. You'll see.

BABY: You mustn't Tommie.

TOMMIE: You did! Why can't I? Sophie always says I'm
slow. And Mr Vogel says I'm lazy. And sometimes he beats
me.

BABY: I know…it's not easy. When I…went away…with
him…I also thought everything would be better. That I
would be happy. And that all my dreams would come true.
But… After a while…things began to change. It wasn't…as
I thought. He wasn't…how I thought he'd be. He was
always angry…and smelling of communion wine.

TOMMIE: What do you mean?

BABY: It…doesn't matter any more. Don't ask me any more.
I don't…want to tell you…about these things. (*Passionately.*)
It's a dangerous world out there Tommie. For people like
you and me. I know…you're not happy to stay here. But
you're safe. Believe me. Please promise me you won't run
away. Promise.

TOMMIE: I promise. But I don't want to.
(*SOPHIE and MINNIE appear in the doorway. SOPHIE has
her arm around MINNIE, who looks rather woeful.*)

SOPHIE: Minnie…felt a little under the weather. It is slaving
over a hot stove. It's never good for her. But now she feels
much better, isn't that so Minnie?

MINNIE: Yes.

(*SOPHIE leads MINNIE to the table and pushes her down on the chair.*)

SOPHIE: Did the two of you have a nice little talk? I'm so glad. (*Short silence. As if having a sudden idea.*) Tommie, did you fasten the back gate with a wire?

TOMMIE: I…don't know.

SOPHIE: You mustn't be negligent, Tommie. That pit-bull bitch will get into the garden and dig up all our bulbs. Do it at once!

TOMMIE: But Sophie…

SOPHIE: I won't ask again!

(*TOMMIE exits towards the kitchen. BABY gets up and attempts to follow TOMMIE. SOPHIE stops her.*)

Sit down Baby. (*Pushes BABY down in a chair.*) Sit down. It's time we had a little talk, don't you think so? High time. (*BABY remains silent and averts her eyes.*)

All these years…I've kept my silence. I've kept… everything in here. (*Makes a fist and knocks against her chest. It makes a hollow sound.*) In…here.

MINNIE: (*Bursting out.*) It's because Ma wouldn't let her! Not a word! She wouldn't hear anything against you! Because you've always been her pet!

SOPHIE: Come now, Minnie…

MINNIE: Yes…yes you have! New dresses for you and Sophie's hand-me-downs for me!

SOPHIE: Come Minnie. This is quite unnecessary.

MINNIE: We couldn't say a thing. You caused us so much suffering and misery and we couldn't even complain!

SOPHIE: Minnie, be quiet! As I was saying…it's time that all these things came out. A closed wound festers, as the old people used to say. Isn't that true Baby? It's time we spoke…of what happened…between you…and him. For many years we've been silent. But now it's time. (*MINNIE whimpers.*)

Let me not beat about the bush. Let me speak his name now plainly and openly. After all…this time. I'm not afraid to say it.

(*MINNIE closes her ears with her hands and screws up her eyes.*)

(*SOPHIE opens her mouth wide and attempts to form a syllable. She is unable to do so. She tries again in an agonizing way. Suddenly she succeeds. She speaks the name loudly and hurriedly.*) Albinus Schiffermiller. Albinus Schiffermiller!

(*MINNIE whimpers loudly.*)

(*Turns her head away. Clearly very distressed.*) That man! We opened our home to him. We trusted him, even if he was a foreigner.

(*SOPHIE and MINNIE are clearly very upset.*)

BABY: (*Speaks slowly with heart-rending sadness.*) Albinus Schiffermiller...Albinus...I remember...in the evening... he would sit at this table...he would sit here... (*Points.*) and our father...over there. (*Points.*) They would talk about...marble...and wreathes...father...would fill in order forms... I would sit quietly...and pretend not to notice him. Every now and then...he would look at me. I could... feel him looking at me.

MINNIE: (*Bursting out.*) How can you! Don't you have any shame!

BABY: And when I turned my head...I'd see him smiling at me with his eyes and stroking his moustache...

MINNIE: Sophie, why don't you stop her!

SOPHIE: She needs to get this off her chest. It would be better...if she told us everything.

BABY: And I...wanted to look at him...but I couldn't. I would look...at everything else. Through the window...at the sun setting...at the papers on the table...at father's hand... covered in grey flannel...

SOPHIE: I'd almost forgotten. Grey cloth wrapped around his right hand because of the eczema. Poor father. As if he was...repelled by life's unclean touch... (*She is tearful and puts her hand in front of her eyes.*) Go on Baby. Tell us everything. The truth will set you free.

BABY: One evening...we passed each other near the outhouse...and he asked if I would wait for him under the pear tree... He said...I should slip out without anyone seeing...

SOPHIE: That wicked, wicked man.

BABY: I could feel my shoes…getting wet…and my feet were cold…but I didn't care. I stayed there until he said goodnight to our father and came out into the yard. But just then…*you* ran after him. (*Points at SOPHIE.*)
(*SOPHIE gasps.*)
You asked if you could go for a walk with him. Because the air was so fresh after the rain. But he said…

SOPHIE: How dare you? (*Rising.*) I can see now. There is no end to your wickedness. You don't want to confess your own sins! You want to point a finger at others. You dare to imply that I…that I…you dare!!

BABY: But you said I should tell you everything.

SOPHIE: Be quiet. You lying Jezebel!

MINNIE: (*Bursting out at last.*) You little slut! Slut! Slut! Slut, slut, slut!!
(*BABY covers her face with her hands.*)
You horrible…horrible…slut!

SOPHIE: (*Warningly.*) Minnie! (*Draws MINNIE aside.*) We don't want her to go and tell Ma. We don't want that do we? We must work…a little more carefully. Otherwise… we will never be able to do what we have to. (*Over-friendly. Approaching BABY.*) We're sorry Baby…we didn't mean to say these things to you. Isn't that true Minnie? Isn't that true?

MINNIE: Yes.

SOPHIE: Believe me. We don't want to hurt your feelings. We only want what is best for you. We don't want you to be tormented…and unhappy. We want you…to come to rest. To know…peace at last. We want that with all our hearts. Come now Baby…don't sulk. Look at me. I didn't mean to be unkind. It's…the sudden heat. And the sweet smell of the flowering creeper. So strong and sweet. I can't get any sleep. I keep waking up…because I have such terrible dreams. Let's forget what happened a moment ago. We won't think about it any more. This is no time for disagreement. Isn't that so Minnie?
(*Small choking sound from MINNIE.*)
Because you see…Baby, there is…something we must talk

to you about. Something very serious. You see Baby…this is not your home any longer.

BABY: (*Confused.*) But why?

SOPHIE: This is not where you belong. I know it is difficult to understand but I'll try and explain.

BABY: This is my home. And I'd promised Ma that I'd always come back.

SOPHIE: Don't misunderstand me. It's not that we don't want you here. It's just…that you wouldn't be here…if you'd been…virtuous. You're only here now…because you stumbled…because…you took a wrong turn.

BABY: But I didn't! I didn't! I came straight here!

SOPHIE: (*Sighs deeply.*) You don't seem…to understand. Now…how should I explain? The truth is Baby…you need to be released. Released from all your pain and suffering. And then you'll be free…to go away from this place. And never to return.

BABY: I don't want that!

SOPHIE: That's only…because you've been blinded by your own wickedness.

(*MINNIE starts crying.*)

Because…you've not repented.

(*MINNIE starts sobbing loudly.*)

Because you've not asked for forgiveness!

MINNIE: (*Bursting out.*) Your wickedness!

SOPHIE: Be quiet Minnie! Be quiet.

MINNIE: I won't be quiet! I won't! For twelve years I had to keep quiet…and I can't any more!

SOPHIE: Come now Minnie…you're going to spoil everything!

MINNIE: If I only think…of this life… If I only think…for twelve years…no one ever visiting us…except Hannah Vlok… For twelve years we could never leave this house!

SOPHIE: Forgive her Baby. Since her ovaries were removed she becomes easily overwrought.

MINNIE: Only to church…where the people move away when we sit down…

SOPHIE: Come now Minnie! Baby has suffered enough!

MINNIE: Or to the shop…where the people fall quiet when we come in. And all because of you!

SOPHIE: Stop it! Baby has enough to endure!

MINNIE: Endure? She doesn't endure anything! Just look at her…pretty and young! And what about me? What about my suffering. My terrible headaches! My festering wound!

SOPHIE: Minnie! I won't hear another word! (*Glares at MINNIE.*) You see Baby…if you only had remorse…you would be free to go…and enter…

MINNIE: (*Bitterly.*) Endure!

BABY: And will I never come back again?

SOPHIE: (*Ecstatic.*) But you wouldn't want to, my dear sister! You wouldn't want to! You would know bliss and rest and eternal peace!

BABY: But I don't want that!

SOPHIE: (*Shocked.*) You don't know what you're saying! (*MINNIE is crying softly now and constantly wiping her eyes.*)

BABY: This is my house and I belong here. I belong here! This is where I belong!

SOPHIE: Poor deluded soul! You don't belong here any more. Believe me!

BABY: (*Eyes shining.*) I do! When I'm asleep…I dream of being here. From afar I can see all the lights in the houses…shining like stars. And the thin church steeple… pointing at the moon. Slowly…I get closer and closer… until I'm at the top of our street…and I can see cats crouching in the shadows…and smell the blossoms of the lemon trees. Then…I go through the gate…into the back yard…the earth is damp…and soft between my toes. And the wet blossoms…touch my hair and my face. Then…I go to the window of Ma's room…I put my fingers…against the glass.

MINNIE: You unclean thing! Lurking in the darkness! Haunting the living!

BABY: Inside…the candle is burning! Ma is lying in bed…she's asleep…she's forgotten to blow it out…she's sleeping...and dreaming of me. And of the garden...of the trees...and the birds...

MINNIE: Nothing has changed...

BABY: And when I get into the house...I see the big, black kettle on the stove...

MINNIE: (*Softly.*) It's still the same...

BABY: And I smell...linoleum and paraffin...

MINNIE: (*Softly.*) It's not right...

BABY: Yes! This is my house! For always! Since I can remember...I've heard the church bells ringing.

MINNIE: (*Louder.*) Everything for her and nothing for us.

BABY: And the old black kettle singing on the stove...

MINNIE: (*Louder.*) Look at her. Her face shining with pleasure! Happy and healthy! What do you say now Sophie? Where is her suffering? And look at us! Thin and pale and forgotten...in this haunted house! Maybe she is the blessed and we are the damned!

SOPHIE: Oh...my heart shudders in my breast...and I am mortally afraid!

MINNIE: You are wrong Sophie! (*Laughs wildly and hysterically.*) *She* is not being punished for anything! It's *us*! We've been condemned to purgatory!

SOPHIE: It is terrible. It is horrible! Our own sister...I don't even want to say it...but I have to! (*Points a finger at BABY.*) She is an instrument of the dark powers! She brings darkness into this house! The darkness of doubt! She will tempt us...into mortal sin! She will let us believe...that goodness will not be rewarded...and that sinfulness will not be condemned!

(*BABY looks very frightened and backs away from SOPHIE.*)

MINNIE: You're wrong Sophie...can't you see! There is no justice! (*Storms out to the passage.*)

SOPHIE: (*Following her.*) Don't be tempted...by this atrocity! You're being led astray! Minnie! (*Calling from the passage door.*) Led astray! Beware Minnie! Beware! You will plunge into the abyss! (*Exits.*)

MINNIE: (*Off.*) I'm afraid Sophie. I'm afraid!

SOPHIE: (*Off.*) Don't be, Minnie. You must listen to me.

(*A soft muttering can be heard indistinctly and further away.
As soon as SOPHIE leaves the room, BABY looks for a way to
escape. She runs into MA's room.*)

BABY: Ma. Ma!

(*MA doesn't respond and appears to be deeply asleep. BABY looks
at her for a moment, then goes to the bedroom window and looks
out as if she has become aware of something outside.*)

SOPHIE: (*Off. Louder.*) Nothing can overcome us. But you
must do what I tell you.

(*BABY becomes aware of the danger. Just as SOPHIE appears
in the passage door, with MINNIE behind her, BABY dashes
into the living room. She sees SOPHIE and runs towards the
outside door.*)

No! You don't! Minnie, she's trying to get away! (*Rushes
towards BABY and grabs her by her arm. She drags her to the
middle of the room.*) Repent Baby! Repent! (*Pushes her roughly
onto her knees.*) The sooner you do it, the better!

BABY: You're hurting me!

SOPHIE: Help me Minnie! (*To BABY.*) Repent, repent! And
we'll be rid of you! Minnie! Pull yourself together! Help
me!

BABY: (*Wriggling.*) No! Let me go!

SOPHIE: Minnie!!

(*MINNIE approaches.*)

Minnie, press her hands together!

(*MINNIE kneels in front of BABY and starts trying to press
her hands together.*)

Now say after me! 'I am a vile and sinful creature!' Say it!

BABY: I won't! (*Starts sobbing.*)

SOPHIE: Say it! (*Gives a resounding slap on her cheek.*)

I won't ask you again!

MINNIE: She's hurting me!

SOPHIE: Be quiet! Now say it! 'I am...'

BABY: No! No!

SOPHIE: (*Starts winding BABY's hair around her hand.*) You...
will...do...as...I...say! (*Pulls her hair.*)

(*BABY cries out. SOPHIE slowly and remorselessly pulls her
hair. BABY's head moves back.*)

Now say after me! I am...

TOMMIE: (*Appearing in the back door.*) What are you doing? You're hurting Baby!

BABY: Tommie! Help me!

SOPHIE: Go to your room! Go!

TOMMIE: I won't! I'll go and tell Ma! (*Runs towards MA's room and exits.*)

MINNIE: He'll tell Ma…

SOPHIE: It doesn't matter any more! Nothing matters! We are attacked by 'powers and principalities'! Stay where you are Minnie!

(*MINNIE whimpers but keeps holding BABY's hands together.*)

No wait! Get the holy water Minnie! It's next to the bread tin! Then you'll see how it blisters her skin! Then you'll see! Then you'll see!

(*A sudden agonized cry from TOMMIE. TOMMIE appears in the doorway. He looks extremely distressed.*)

TOMMIE: It's Ma! It's Ma! I thought she was asleep…I tried to wake her…but…Ma!!! She won't wake up! She won't wake up!

(*MINNIE covers her mouth with her hands.*)

(*Covers his head with his hands.*) Ma!!

SOPHIE: (*Pushes BABY aside. Hisses.*) I'll deal with you later. (*Gets up and goes to MA's room.*)

(*SOPHIE pushes past TOMMIE and goes to MA's bed. The lights fade up in MA's room.*)

Ma! Ma! (*Shakes her lightly. SOPHIE kneels down and puts her head on MA's chest. She listens for a time. She rises slowly.*) Yes…

TOMMIE: What's wrong with Ma? Why doesn't she wake up?

(*MINNIE has now approached and also stands in the doorway looking into MA's room. Lights up on MA's room and dim on the living room.*)

SOPHIE: (*Turns around slowly.*) I'm afraid…you must be strong…but Ma…has left this world.

(*MINNIE starts moaning. Her moans start rising and threaten to turn into hysteria. TOMMIE rushes to MA's bed and falls down next to it.*)

TOMMIE: Ma! Ma! Ma!

SOPHIE: Stop it Minnie! And don't blabber Tommie! Try to behave like a man. (*She turns around and closes MA's eyes. She pulls the sheet over MA's head.*)

TOMMIE: No! (*Takes the sheet off.*)

(*SOPHIE folds MA's hands on her chest. TOMMIE starts keening. He rests his arms on the bed and puts his head in his arms. This sound continues until otherwise indicated in the text. MINNIE suddenly starts wailing in a high voice. SOPHIE rushes up to her and slaps her.*)

SOPHIE: Stop it! We don't have time for this!

(*MINNIE stops it.*

As SOPHIE continues to speak to MINNIE, BABY very slowly gets up. She seems to be listening to something in the back garden. Now we can also hear a very soft flapping sound. Like wings. Or wet washing on a washing line blowing in the wind. She moves softly to the back door. She looks out through the gauze into the garden. She remains like this until otherwise indicated in the text.)

We have a lot to do, do you hear me Minnie?

MINNIE: Yes…

SOPHIE: That's better. Go and find a sheet and cover the mirror in the passage.

MINNIE: (*Tearful again.*) Yes Sophie…

SOPHIE: (*Calls after MINNIE.*) And then you will have to go to Mr Vogel and tell him about Ma. When the doctor has been here they must come and fetch her. They must take her down to the cellar. Do you hear me? Don't just stand there!

MINNIE: (*Hurrying off towards the bedroom.*) Yes Sophie!

SOPHIE: (*Puts her hand on TOMMIE's shoulders.*) Be brave Tommie. Be brave. (*Hurries after MINNIE.*) And tell him we will come and choose a coffin tomorrow! Sensible and durable and not too expensive! And I'll go and call the doctor and tell the minister on my way back! (*Suddenly seeing the remains of the birthday party on the table.*) Good heavens! Just look at this! I completely forgot! Minnie! Come and help me! Minnie!

(*MINNIE appears in the passage door. Lights up on the living room.*)

We will have to clean up before the minister and the doctor arrive. What will they think of us?

(*While SOPHIE continues to speak MINNIE and SOPHIE remove everything from the table and carry it to the kitchen. There is a very rapid to-ing and fro-ing from the living room to the kitchen and sometimes SOPHIE's voice can be heard from the kitchen. But other times she calls after MINNIE as MINNIE disappears into the kitchen.*)

I hope the funeral isn't too soon. We'll have to do a lot of baking. And of course, we need two black dresses and Tommie needs a black suit. And we will have to get something decent for Ma to wear for the showing. Don't spill Minnie! And hurry up! Salty things are best. I never think sweet things are fitting for a funeral. Don't dawdle! And wipe the table!

MINNIE: Yes Sophie.

SOPHIE: And while you finish…I'll go and fetch my handbag and put on my hat. (*Moves towards the passage door and exits.*)
(*MINNIE brings a damp cloth and start wiping the table.*)

SOPHIE: (*Off.*) Oh yes…Minnie you must go and find Ma's documents! The doctor will need them for the death certificate!

MINNIE: Where are they?

SOPHIE: (*Off.*) In the biscuit tin! In her top drawer!
(*MINNIE finishes wiping the table and hurries off towards MA's room. She averts her eyes from MA's still form and goes towards the bureau. She opens the drawers. TOMMIE hardly notices her. He is now keening very softly. While MINNIE is off, BABY opens the side door and goes into the back yard. She can vaguely be seen among the trees. Then she disappears. MINNIE opens the drawer then opens the tin and takes out documents. She takes out a piece of paper and looks at it. SOPHIE appears in the living room. She is wearing a small black hat and carrying a handbag over her arm.*)

Minnie. Haven't you done yet?
(*MINNIE enters from MA's room.*)

MINNIE: I have her birth certificate.

SOPHIE: Give it to me.

MINNIE: And I also found this.

SOPHIE: What is it?

MINNIE: (*Reading.*) 'Last Will and Testament of Magdalena Roos.'

SOPHIE: Give it here! Let me see! (*She snatches it away from MINNIE.*)

MINNIE: (*Looks over her shoulder.*) What does it say? Tell me. (*SOPHIE continues to read. She becomes more and more alarmed.*)

SOPHIE: (*Pale and shaken.*) Oh…oh…I feel so…dizzy… (*Sits down on a chair at the table.*) My legs…are giving way…

MINNIE: (*Alarmed.*) What is it Sophie?

SOPHIE: My poor sister… (*Drops her head in her hands and moans softly and repetitively.*) My poor sister…I don't know… how to tell you…

MINNIE: You're frightening me Sophie.

SOPHIE: (*Moans and moans.*) It's the end. It's the end for us. (*Moaning.*)

MINNIE: Speak to me. (*She takes the will from SOPHIE and reads it.*)

SOPHIE: Oh my sister…what will become of us? We have been cast…into outer darkness. (*Moans rhythmically.*)

MINNIE: (*Unbelievingly.*) The house…and everything in it…belongs to him!

SOPHIE: (*Wildly and near hysteria.*) To that simpleton!

MINNIE: (*Reading.*) 'Shall leave the said premises…in no less than…one month…'

SOPHIE: To be kicked out of our own home! Treated like dogs! The home that belonged to our father!

MINNIE: (*Tearful.*) Father should never have left everything to her! He should never have trusted that woman!

SOPHIE: But it was the right and proper thing to do. Father always did his duty. (*Moans rhythmically.*) Poor father! He must be turning in his grave!

MINNIE: We get…'the mortuary…and the funeral concern'.

SOPHIE: (*Now weeping helplessly.*) We will wander about…like
lost souls. Homeless wanderers. Far away from here…
where nobody knows us. Where nobody knows…our
shame. Even…the fox has a hole…but what do we have?
No place to call our own?

MINNIE: (*Slightly hysterical.*) But we don't know anywhere
else! We'll be lost! Lost in the dark!
(*For a few moments the sisters keen and cry together. Then
MINNIE wipes her nose. She seems to be thinking.*)
But Sophie…what will happen…if nobody sees this.

SOPHIE: You stupid thing…there are witnesses. (*Prods the
will.*) Can't you see? Hannah Vlok and that slimy son of
hers!

MINNIE: But…if it is lost. If no one can find it?

SOPHIE: What do you mean? Minnie! What are you
thinking?

MINNIE: I mean…who would know the difference?

SOPHIE: (*Grandly. Pointing a finger.*) There is an eye that never
sleeps! Do you want to be eternally damned?

MINNIE: I mean…Tommie won't be able to polish the
linoleum…or shine the pots…or iron the sheets. It would
be much better for him…if we stayed. And who else would
cook sweet pumpkin for him? Or mashed beans and
potato?

SOPHIE: Well…if you put it like that…I suppose…I mean…
we do keep everything spick and span…and who else
would clean the house? And see that he wears a hat in the
sun. You might be right Minnie…you might…be right.
It could certainly…be the best thing. I don't know what
that woman was thinking! That wicked woman! Our own
father's house! To steal it from us and give it to him! That's
not justice.

MINNIE. You're right Sophie! It's wicked!

SOPHIE: Yes…maybe we should just forget about this.

MINNIE: (*Whispering. Looking around furtively.*) What should
we do with it? Should we…hide it?

SOPHIE: No…no… (*Thinking.*)

(*BABY appears at the outside door. She can be seen through the gauze.*)

I know…we can burn it in the stove!

MINNIE: Yes! That's a good idea.

SOPHIE: You must go and draw the kitchen curtains.

(*MINNIE hurries towards the kitchen and exits. The strange flapping sound is heard again.*)

What was that? (*She stands motionless.*) I must go and lock the front door. (*Puts the will on the table and hurries off to the passage.*)

(*BABY enters silently. She snatches the will from the table and hides it behind her back.*)

(*Entering and not seeing the will.*) It must be completely reduced to ashes, Minnie. Not a scrap left behind!

MINNIE: (*Appears in the kitchen door.*) What do you mean, Sophie?

SOPHIE: The will. Are you burning it?

MINNIE: But I thought you had it.

SOPHIE: Stupid woman! What are you saying? How can it disappear into thin air?

(*SOPHIE and MINNIE notice BABY. They both give a start.*)

MINNIE: I thought you'd gone! Where did you come from?

SOPHIE: (*Suddenly realizing.*) It's her! She's taken it! Give it back to us. Give it at once! At once!

(*BABY shakes her head and retreats from SOPHIE.*)

(*Enraged.*) Oh…oh…I could…tear you to pieces!

(*As SOPHIE rushes towards BABY, there is a loud knock off.*)

MINNIE: (*Urgent whisper.*) Someone at the kitchen door.

SOPHIE: (*Hissing.*) See who it is and send them away.

(*MINNIE hurries off to the kitchen. SOPHIE remains motionless glaring at BABY. Voices can be heard from the kitchen, then the sound of a door being closed. MINNIE appears in the kitchen.*)

MINNIE: It was Hannah Vlok.

SOPHIE: What did she want?

MINNIE: She asked what all the commotion was about. I told her. She started weeping and ran off to call the minister.

SOPHIE: Busybody! Old vulture! (*Turning back to BABY.*) Give it to me! I'm getting very angry!
(*She moves towards BABY. BABY keeps shaking her head.*)
(*Beside herself.*) I'll kill you! I'll kill you! As God is my witness I'll kill you!
(*BABY darts away from SOPHIE.*)
You'll be sorry!! (*SOPHIE clumsily chases BABY. Her hands are stretched out in front of her. She is in a terrible rage, snarling and hissing. She bumps into a chair and it falls over. She stumbles and falls. Her hat is knocked off.*)

MINNIE: Sophie! Sophie! Stop it!
(*SOPHIE turns to MINNIE in shocked surprise.*)
(*Sympathetically.*) Maybe...you should...go and call the doctor. The minister will be here soon. And...what will he think?
(*SOPHIE clenches her fists. Her tightly coiled bun has come undone. Her face is distorted in a terrible grimace. She gives a choked, almost soundless cry. Then, suddenly her face goes slack. She gets up very slowly. She looks pale, hunched and defeated.*)
(*Picks up the hat almost tenderly.*) Come Sophie... Come.
(*Puts on the hat for SOPHIE.*) We have things to do.
(*MINNIE leads SOPHIE to the passage door. SOPHIE shuffles like a very old woman.*)

SOPHIE: (*Turning at the door. Her face twisted with hatred. To BABY.*) You might think you got the better of us. But there is a...a higher justice! (*Her voice cracking.*) A higher justice!
(*SOPHIE and MINNIE exit. A moment later the sound of the front door opening and closing.*
BABY goes to MA's room. The lights dim in the living room. She stands behind TOMMIE. He is still crying softly, his head in his arms.)

BABY: Tommie. Tommie.
(*TOMMIE looks around. He wipes his nose on the back of his arm.*)
(*Giving him the will.*) Ma wants you to keep this. You must give it to the doctor when he comes. To no one else. There. (*Puts it in his coat pocket.*) Did you hear me?

(*TOMMIE nods. TOMMIE turns away again. He wipes his eyes with his knuckles.*)

(*Tenderly.*) Don't cry.

TOMMIE: Ma is gone. She said she would never leave me. Said...she would watch over me. She promised. But now...she's gone. (*Cries.*) She's left me alone. And...she'll never come back.

BABY: (*Softly.*) No. You're wrong. She'll never break a promise. You know that.

TOMMIE: She's broken this one! She's...gone.

BABY: No. She's here. She is.

TOMMIE: Where is she? I can't see her.

(*BABY goes to the window and looks out.*)

BABY: Look out there.

TOMMIE: I don't want to see anything. (*Looks at MA.*) If I call her she won't answer. (*Sobs.*)

BABY: Come and see.

TOMMIE: (*Getting up slowly.*) Where?

(*BABY points.*)

(*Stands next to her and looks out.*) I can't see anything.

BABY: Look in the branches up there!

TOMMIE: I can't see.

BABY: There. (*Points.*) On the end of the big branch.

TOMMIE: Yes! (*Disappointed.*) It's just a night bird.

BABY: See how its eyes are shining. And can you...see... how the moon slides between the thin clouds...and the shadow of leaves against the wall of the outhouse? And the irises so white in the moonlight and the ranunculus wet and heavy and hanging their heads?

TOMMIE: Yes...

BABY: And...you watch very carefully...you can also see... Ma.

TOMMIE: (*In disbelief.*) I...can?

BABY: Yes. You must believe me. Maybe in the...deep shadows of the pepper tress or...near the water tank...or just disappearing around the corner of the house.

TOMMIE: Really?

BABY: It's true. I've never ever lied to you, have I?

(*TOMMIE shakes his head.*)

And even…when you can't see her…you must know that she's there. She's always near. Looking after you.

TOMMIE: Can she see me?

BABY: Yes. Even without her glasses.

TOMMIE: Will she hear me when I talk to her?

BABY: Yes. She can hear…even the smallest thing. She can even hear…your heart beating.

TOMMIE: Can she?

BABY: (*Softly.*) Yes.

(*With wonderment TOMMIE slowly puts his hand on his heart. As TOMMIE continues to stand at the window looking out, BABY leaves the room soundlessly and crosses the living room to the outside door. The living room is very dimly lit and the blossom trees can be seen through the back wall. As BABY reaches the outside door, the single door of the heavy cupboard creaks ominously open. There is a light focused on the cupboard which now reveals its interior. It is a cold, greenish light. It reveals a black tail-coat over a white shirt – resembling the trunk and arms of a dismembered body – hanging behind the cupboard door as well as three top hats arranged in a row on a shelf. As the door creaks open, BABY turns around and watches with horror. For a time she seems almost transfixed by what she sees. Then she moves to the cupboard, hesitates only for a moment, then firmly closes the cupboard door turning the key in the lock. When she turns around, there is a look of delight on her face. Lightly she moves to the outside door and exits, noiselessly closing the door behind her. At moments her slight figure can be seen between the trees before she disappears. The lights fade out in the living room. Only MA's room is dimly lit. Bright moonlight falls through the window onto TOMMIE's face.*)

TOMMIE: Ma! Can you see me? It's Tommie! Here, at the window. Ma, I'll leave the windows open… And the curtains. Even when it rains… Even when the wind blows… So you can see me. So you can see that your Tommie…is polishing his shoes…and putting all his things in the right place. And that your Tommie…is eating all his vegetables and washing his face every morning. And

even when I go to bed. I'll leave the candle burning. Not because I'm scared of the dark. But so you can see me when I sleep. So...you can watch me... until the...sun... comes up...behind the vegetable garden...
(*As TOMMIE continues to look dreamily into the back garden, the lights fade very slowly to black.*)

BREATHING IN

Characters

ANNA
a travelling herbalist and wise woman. Middle-aged.
She is very unpredictable. Her age and even her
appearance seem to change from time to time

ANNIE
her fragile daughter. She is pale with very long, red
hair. It is difficult to determine her age

BRAND
although he seems gaunt and worn-out,
he is fairly young

THE GENERAL
middle-aged. A tough, sinewy man.
Now hollow-eyed and feverish

Accent
These characters are not English-speaking South
Africans, but Afrikaners and as such a 'South African'
accent is not required. 'Normal' English can be used,
since the convention is that the characters are speaking
Afrikaans.

Breathing In was first staged in July 2005 by the Baxter Theatre, Rhodes University, The National Arts Festival and The First Physical Theatre Company at the Box Theatre in Grahamstown, with the following cast:

ANNA, Antoinette Kellerman

ANNIE, Jenny Stead

BRAND, Ashley Waterman

GENERAL, Mark Hoeben

Directed and designed by Marthinus Basson

It subsequently transferred to The Baxter Theatre in Cape Town where it opened in July of the same year.

My sincere thanks to Rhodes University, The Baxter Theatre, The National Arts Festival and The First Physical Theatre Company for their support. More particularly to Marthinus Basson and his cast for a wickedly evocative and utterly superb production.

Set

Time Evening. Early winter towards the end of the Anglo-Boer war.

Setting A cowshed on a desolate farm.

Set Two big doors left back form the entrance to the cowshed. Middle left centre, a small wood-burning stove. Next to the stove are a few logs and a poker. Near the stove a bench and a wooden arm-chair, once beautiful, but now partly scorched as if it has been rescued from a fire. Also an upturned crate with pots and cooking utensils on it, as well as a jar of honey, a small bowl, a cup and an enamel coffee-pot. Middle centre a rough-hewn table with a bench upstage. On the table, a pestle and mortar, herbs, a long knife, a large bowl, a jug and a cloth. Right of the table a green chair. It is narrow with a high back. A harness, with worn leather straps and brass buckles is fastened to it. Right back a few bales of straw. Right middle there is a wooden feeding trough. On top of the trough there is a tin trunk with its lid open. Front right, broadside on, there is a wooden feeding trough which serves as the General's bed. A rusted shovel and a hay-fork lean next to the shed door. There is a large hook on the doorpost. Candles are burning on the crate, the table, and a single candle next to the General's 'bed'.

Lighting The set should be very dimly lit. Small pools of warm light around the candles form a contrast with the grey, powdery light suffusing the set.

ACT ONE

As the play starts, there is the sound of soft, soaking rain. The GENERAL is asleep. He is lying on straw and is covered by animal skins. ANNIE is strapped into the green chair. She is staring front. She is wearing a worn and patched dress. ANNA enters, leaving the barn door slightly open. The sound of the soaking rain becomes louder. ANNA is wet and dishevelled. Her hands are covered in mud and the hem of her dun-coloured dress is mud stained. She is carrying a small sack which is almost empty.

ANNA: I haven't been away for too long have I? At least the
fire hasn't gone out. (*Goes over to the stove, throwing the sack
on the table in passing.*) I'm so wet and cold. And muddy.
But better for it to be wet when I dig for roots. Didn't
find many. Pitch dark. And slippery. (*Touches her hair.*) I
even have mud in my hair. (*Goes to the stove.*) He didn't
leave us very much wood did he? Not even enough to last
the night. (*Strange little smile.*) But then… that won't be
necessary. (*Puts a log on the stove.*) You mustn't worry my
girl. Everything is going to be all right. Have I ever lied to
you? (*Stokes the fire with a poker.*) Have I ever?

ANNIE: (*Quietly.*) No, mother.

ANNA: You see! When I get the feeling here… (*Touches her
abdomen.*) and here… (*Touches her forehead.*) Then I know
that there is nothing to fear. Have I ever been wrong in all
these years?

(*The GENERAL groans.*)

Did he wake up when I was gone?

ANNIE: No mother.

ANNA: That's because I made him a good, strong brew.
(*Bends down and blows into the fire.*) I found some more roots
to put in the pot. I don't want any trouble from him. (*Closes
the stove door. Now soothing, half crooning.*) It will still be a
little while, my girl. But not too long. Not too long. (*Looks
at ANNIE and sees that she is falling asleep. Screams suddenly.*)
Open your eyes! (*Rushes to ANNIE.*) Keep awake! (*Leans
over ANNIE with her face almost touching ANNIE's. Quietly
and ominously.*) You mustn't. You mustn't. You're so terribly

pale. Look at the circles under your eyes. (*Lifts her hand.*)
Your hands are so cold. No blood in your hands. (*Holds her
hand up to the candle flame.*) And so thin. I can see the flame
right through the skin. (*Crooning again.*) But don't you fret
now. It won't be long. Not long. You'll soon have colour
in your cheeks again, my girl. My poor little girl. You'll be
strong again. (*Suddenly curt.*) Say: 'Yes mother.'

ANNIE: Yes mother.

ANNA: There you are. (*Steps back and looks at ANNIE with
narrowed eyes.*) We'll have to dress you very nicely.

ANNIE: No, please. I don't want to.

ANNA: (*Curtly.*) You have to get ready. You know that very
well.

ANNIE: I'm tired. I feel so worn out.

ANNA: There now. (*Croons again.*) I'll help. I'll dress you.
You'll hardly have to do a thing. I'll button you up and I'll
brush your hair. (*Quietly and suggestively.*) You know how
they always love your hair.

ANNIE: Can't you please leave me alone. Please…please
leave me alone. I don't want this any more.

ANNA: You don't know what you're saying. You silly, stupid
ungrateful girl! After all I've done for you!

ANNIE: I don't want everything to be the same. Over…and
over…and over again. Leave me alone… (*Long breath out as
her head sags forward.*) …I'm too tired.

ANNA: (*Lifts her head by her hair.*) Stop it now! Just stop it! And
what would I do without you? (*Suddenly kind and cajoling.*)
Think of your poor mother. What would I do? Come
now… (*Lifts her chin.*) Don't be sad. Give us a smile.
(*ANNIE gives a watery smile.*)
There we are! That's better. (*Gives a little shriek.*) Oh you
should have reminded me! I must put on the coffee. The
fire is burning so low, it'll take forever to boil. (*Sighs.*)
Forever. I'll give him some coffee when he gets here. He'll
be wet through and very tired. (*Scoffing.*) And not what
they call coffee these days. Scorched mealie cobs. Not that.
He'll be so pleased. (*Smiles slyly.*) That's why we always
have to keep nice things. To please them. To make them

feel at ease. (*Suddenly upset. Shivers.*) A draft going down my back. Like thin fingers touching me. I've left the door open again. (*Rushes to the door and slams it shut. Walks back to the fire very slowly. Seems suddenly exhausted and much older.*) Not that it helps much. With all the leaks in the roof. Cracks in the walls. And smelling of rats. (*Cajoling.*) But never mind. We'll soon be back in our wagon. High and dry above the ground. Safe and sound and going far away from here. (*ANNIE's head droops and her eyes close.*)

(*Noticing this.*) Sit up! Sit up! You're not going to sleep are you? You mustn't! (*Menacingly, moving towards ANNIE.*) You mustn't! You know that you'll never wake up again. You know…that you won't. (*With slowly growing terror.*) You'll slip away and I'll never find you again. (*Crouches down in front of ANNIE.*) I'll never find you again! (*Puts her arms around ANNIE and holds her very tightly.*) My little Annie…my little girl…all I have in the world. You're everything to me. If you leave me behind, I'll be all alone. All alone. (*Gives a long moan. Short silence. Gets up very slowly. She seems suddenly tired and defeated.*) So you must keep your eyes…wide open, my girl. (*Very slowly.*) Open…wide…and let me see.

(*ANNIE opens her eyes very wide.*)

Yes. Keep them like that then you'll stay awake. (*Sits down heavily on the bench at the table.*) It's also this rain. This endless rain. Making you drowsy. (*Sighs. Drops her face in her hands.*) It's…tiring me out as well. All my bones are aching… And these last days…I've been feeling so…funny. I've had aches…and pains everywhere. And sometimes… everything seems to grow dim and I hardly know where I am. Then I had a dream of hands…growing out of the earth. Wanting to pull me down. (*Comfortingly.*) Oh, but I don't want to scare you my girl. I'm sure it's nothing. I'm sure. You know me.

GENERAL: (*Talking in his sleep.*) Take cover! Here they come! Here they come! (*Mumbles inaudibly. He continues to mumble until otherwise indicated in the text.*)

ANNA: Let him dream, poor thing. That's all that's left for
him now.

ANNIE: (*Shuddering.*) But such terrible dreams about fighting
and killing.

GENERAL: (*Talking in his sleep.*) Hold your fire! Hold your
fire!! (*Tosses about as he mumbles. Throws off his blanket
exposing his bare chest. He is muscular and very lean.*)

ANNA: (*Looking at him.*) Well, that's what he has on his mind.
It's war after all. Now don't you start feeling sorry for
him. That won't do, my girl, that won't do. (*More kindly.*)
When he wakes up again, poor thing, I'll give him a nice
strong brew. I'll even sing for him. (*Silence. Keeps looking
at the GENERAL who has stopped muttering and has fallen
deeply asleep again. Musingly.*) He's…a handsome man. I'll
say that for him. Maybe…that's why I've been feeling…so
weak…and so dizzy this evening. Yes…that could be. It's
because he reminds me…he reminds me… (*Claps her hand
over her mouth. Speaks rapidly from behind her hand.*) I don't
want to think about him. I don't want to. I don't want to.
(*Silence. Rises slowly. Moves towards the GENERAL. She moves
slowly and as if compelled against her will. Stands behind the
GENERAL and looks down at him.*) Same strong arms. Same
hands. A real man. But then your father's eyes were black.
Your father had the blackest eyes I've every seen. (*Silence.
Looks down at the GENERAL.*) Seeing him like this…I
can almost imagine…that he is your father…that we are
a family… that we're happy. And that he's sleeping…
because he's tired. He's been chopping wood. Been setting
traps. Been working for us all day. Using his strong hands
to look after us. (*Leans over him and touches his hands. She
turns them over and looks at them. She strokes his palms with
her fingers.*) Just look…at those callouses. (*Voluptuously starts
stroking his bare arms.*) And those…strong arms…

GENERAL: (*Half opens his eyes.*) Get away! Get away! I'll
never surrender!

ANNA: (*Soothingly.*) You go to sleep now. Go to sleep. Shhh…
shhh.

(*The GENERAL mutters. His eyes close again and he falls
asleep. ANNA stands watching him, then almost as if she cannot*

help herself, she bends over him suddenly and kisses him 'upside down' and hard on the mouth.)

(*Suddenly with violent revulsion.*) His breath is rancid! It reeks of fever! (*Wipes the back of her hand over her mouth.*) Well, it's no use dwelling on these things. What is past is past and there's an end to it. After all, we don't have time to waste. We must get you dressed, my girl. I have a feeling…right here… (*Taps her chest.*) …that you need to look your very best tonight. (*Soothingly.*) Not a bad feeling of course. It's just…that everything is getting so difficult these days… even finding a decent pair of shoes. (*Briskly.*) I must wash my hands before I touch the dresses. (*Goes to the bowl. Dips her hand in the water and then rubs her hands with a rough cloth. She goes over to the chest, takes out a flowered dress and puts it back again.*)

(*While ANNA continues to rummage in the chest, ANNIE makes small moaning sounds. At the same time she seems to shudder slightly. To quiver.*)

(*ANNA takes out a white dress and holds it up.*) Yes. This one is right. Pure and simple. You can't go wrong with white.

ANNIE: But I'll be so cold…

ANNA: No, you won't. (*Laughs softly.*) The last time he was in such a hurry that he hardly noticed you. When you're ready he'll hardly be able to believe his eyes. (*Laughs softly.*) This time he'll see you my girl. This time. (*Musingly.*) He's a little thin. But he looks quite healthy. (*Undoes the buckles of the harness.*) I suppose these days you can't ask for too much. At least there's still some life in him. (*Softly.*) Enough. (*Helps ANNIE up.*) Come now. Gently does it. (*Unbuttons her dress. ANNIE sways and seems unsteady on her feet.*)

Poor little girl. Almost dead on your feet. Now lift your arms.

(*ANNIE lifts her arms and ANNA takes off her dress. ANNIE is now dressed in a light petticoat.*)

Keep them up for a little while longer. (*Slips the white dress over her head.*) There you are. (*Crooning, while she sits down on the green chair and takes ANNIE on her lap. She starts buttoning her up.*) Just a few buttons and then we're done. (*Chanting.*)

One two three and four. Now your hair. (*Helps ANNIE up. Gets a brush from the chest and starts brushing her hair.*) Put your head back…
(*ANNIE puts her head back. ANNA brushes her hair in long strokes. With each stroke ANNIE sways a little on her feet.*) There… (*Brushes.*) … There… (*Shudders.*) …your hair is so cold…it slips through my fingers. What a strange feeling it's giving me… (*Shakes her head.*) …Oh, but it's nothing. I'm sure it's nothing. (*Indicates the GENERAL with a head gesture.*) At least he's sleeping peacefully.
(*ANNIE gives a small gasp.*)
Did I hurt you my girl? I'm so sorry. If he's sleeping…that will make a good impression. (*Stops brushing.*) Now let me see. (*Stands back and looks at ANNIE.*) You look so pretty. (*Helps her back onto the green chair.*) Pretty as a picture. (*Moves a few steps towards the stove.*) And the water is almost boiling! (*Claps her hands together.*) Everything is ready. (*Quietly.*) I know he's very close now. Not much time left. (*Emphatically to ANNIE as she moves back to the table.*) When he comes in, you know what to do, don't you? You must lower your eyes. You haven't forgotten have you? You must look very shy. And clasp your hands together in your lap. Don't forget that! Come now! Or would you like me to help you? (*ANNIE clasps her hands on her lap.*)
(*Pleasantly.*) There. It makes you look so much younger. (*Gives a gasp, then hurriedly picks up ANNIE's discarded dress, throws it into the trunk and slams down the lid. Turns round and whispers confidentially.*) And don't put your face too near the candle flame. We don't want him to see that you're not quite as young as you seem. The little lines around your eyes… (*Kindly.*) But don't you worry. You look lovely. (*Muffled sound of horse approaching.*)
(*Triumphantly.*) There he is now! (*Whispering urgently.*) And you don't look up, until I introduce you. You don't want to seem forward. (*ANNA moves towards the door as the sound of the hooves grows louder. She almost reaches the door when she turns around, rushes to ANNIE and pinches her cheeks.*)
ANNIE: You're hurting me!

ANNA: (*Hissing.*) I'm just pinching a little colour into your
cheeks! Shh. (*Holds up her hand. Whispering.*) Here he is.
(*The sound of the hooves has now stopped. ANNA goes to the
door and pushes heavily against it. After a time, BRAND pushes
from the outside, attempting to open the door.*)

BRAND: (*Voice off.*) Open the door! It's Adjutant Brand!
(*ANNA abruptly steps away from the door. The door opens.
BRAND stumbles in. He is wearing a very wet hat and a Mauser
is slung over his shoulder.*)

ANNA: (*Demurely.*) I'm so sorry. I didn't know it was you,
Adjutant.

BRAND: (*Takes off his hat and shakes the water off. Coldly,
indicating the GENERAL.*) And how is he? (*He takes off his
gun.*)

ANNA: As well as can be expected. (*Ingratiating herself. Taking
his gun and hanging it on the hook.*) At least he is sleeping
peacefully. I've been giving him something for the pain.
And I've also put poultices on his wounds to keep it open.
A closed wound can fester so easily.
(*BRAND goes over to the GENERAL and looks at him.*)

BRAND: General! General! It's me, Brand!

ANNA: Let him sleep. He needs to sleep.

BRAND: I have urgent business with him. General!

ANNA: And it's no use now. You'll have to wait a while.
(*Following him. Simpering.*) I told you I'd take care of him,
didn't I? I certainly hope…that you'll give us a little
reward. After all…I have to make a living.

BRAND: You want me to pay you?

ANNA: I have to get by somehow. These are hard times.

BRAND: For nursing the General?

ANNA: (*Very nice.*) And you must get out of that soaking
jacket. You'll catch your death, Adjutant.

BRAND: (*Turns around and looks at her. Passes his hand over
his eyes. Speaks with slow and emphatic disgust.*) Our bravest
General! He's lost his son…his wife…his farm. Everything.
He's given up everything for his fatherland, and you want
me to pay you? (*Shakes his head.*) But what would you
know? General! Please General!

ANNA: (*Timidly.*) I don't understand what you're saying Adjutant? After all…if I perform a service…I should get paid. It's only right, after all.

BRAND: (*Turning around.*) Do you know what we suffer? Never sleeping? Hardly eating? Giving everything we have? But what can I expect from a woman like you? A homeless, rootless wanderer! A parasite!

ANNA: (*Whining.*) Come now. Don't be angry. Won't you have some coffee?

BRAND: You don't know the meaning of patriotism! I don't want anything from you!

ANNA: Well, at least allow me to introduce my daughter. I haven't done it properly.

(*BRAND peers through the darkness and then sees ANNIE. She is looking down very demurely.*)

There she is. Her name is Annie. (*Confidentially.*) She's very shy. She is not used to gentlemen. (*Loudly to ANNIE.*) Say good evening to the Adjutant. He is an important man.

ANNIE: Good evening.

BRAND: Good evening…

ANNA: (*Confidentially. Speaking almost into BRAND's ear.*) She is very…unworldly. Not used to company. Oh, I wish you could see her when she's well. How different she is then. Now she can hardly even stand. And as for walking… Each step causes her such terrible pain. (*Gives a long vocalised sigh.*)

(*BRAND still stands somewhat uncertainly looking at ANNIE.*)

(*Teasing him.*) Come now. Have some coffee. Doesn't it smell delicious. Real coffee. Not much of that around these days. After all, it can't do you any harm.

BRAND: Well, I suppose…

ANNA: (*Pours out the coffee.*) Still quite hot enough. (*Holds the cup out to him.*)

BRAND: (*Takes the coffee.*) Well…thank you.

ANNA: And come and sit here near the fire.

(*BRAND sits on the armchair and drinks his coffee. Silence. From time to time he glances at ANNIE. ANNA watches him.*)

(*Suddenly kneeling in front of him.*) Let me take your shoes off. They'll never dry like that. Nothing is as dangerous as wet shoes.

BRAND: (*Embarrassed.*) Please…

ANNA: Oh…it's no trouble. Just look at them! I can see your toes! You need a nice new pair of boots. I don't even know how you can walk in these.

BRAND: Well, at least I have shoes. Most of the men have nothing left. Bare feet covered in sores.

ANNA: (*Suddenly has a bright idea. Rises.*) I have just what you need! Imagine that! Please excuse me for a while. I must go and find something in the wagon. (*Bustles off.*)
(*Silence.*)

BRAND: (*Glances at ANNIE. He looks straight ahead then glances at her again.*) I'm sorry…if I spoke harshly to your mother. I want you to know…that I'm not usually so impolite. (*Short silence.*) The war…does funny things to one. (*Short silence. Yawns.*) Please forgive me. I'm very tired. I rode for hours to deliver those dispatches. And it's more difficult in the dark.

ANNIE: (*Shyly.*) We also travel at night.

BRAND: Quite right. You shouldn't be seen in daylight. You don't want the enemy to capture you. (*Short silence.*) Your mother…looks after you very well, doesn't she?

ANNIE: She does. She's very good to me. She does everything for me. More than you can think.

BRAND: I'm sure she's a good woman in spite of… everything. (*Stifles a yawn.*)

ANNIE: She is. (*Short silence.*) Are you very sleepy?

BRAND: Yes. I never get enough sleep. Just an hour here and there. And then it's on the hard ground. Or lying in the trenches.

ANNIE: And when you sleep…do you dream?

BRAND: (*Thinking.*) Yes. Sometimes.

ANNIE: And what do you dream about?

BRAND: (*Laugh.*) Food mostly. And soft feather beds.
(*Short silence. ANNIE sighs.*)

ANNIE: I know what I would dream. If I could dream.

BRAND: And can't you?

ANNIE: No. I'm not allowed to go to sleep, you see. My mother keeps me awake. She says that my sleep will be too deep and that I'll fall and fall and never stop. And then I'll leave her behind.

BRAND: (*Confused.*) Oh...

ANNIE: But if I could sleep...I would dream about a big, open field. My mother and I would be sitting outside... looking up at the clear sky.

BRAND: And how do you know that?

ANNIE: (*Smiling secretly.*) Oh, I know. Sometimes...I can almost see it.

BRAND: (*Silence. Embarrassed. Making conversation.*) I suppose...that's why you've not been captured. Because you travel at night. Otherwise...who knows?

ANNIE: But that's not why we travel at night.

BRAND: (*Surprised.*) Not?

ANNIE: No. It's the light. We can't bear the daylight. It hurts us.

BRAND: (*Puzzled.*) I...see.

(*ANNA enters with a pair of shining boots.*)

ANNA: (*To BRAND.*) Here! I think these will do very nicely.

BRAND: (*Shocked.*) But these are...surely...

ANNA: (*Casually.*) I know. Belonged to a fallen enemy soldier.

BRAND: (*Appalled.*) So, you took them off him!

ANNA: Well...I thought they might come in handy. And I was right, wasn't I?

BRAND: What do you take me for?

ANNA: (*Little laugh. Shrugs.*) I should have expected this.

BRAND: (*Jumps up. Completely outraged.*) What do you take me for? I'm not a scavenger! I'm a soldier! Patriot! Defending the honour of my country!

ANNA: Surely you can do that much better if your feet are dry!

BRAND: I would rather die than touch these boots! And you! Get away from me! You carrion crow!

ANNA: (*Innocently. A little outraged.*) A few brass buttons... buckles...pocket watches. What harm can that really do?

(*Suddenly very outraged.*) And what are we supposed to live on? In peacetime we tended to the sick, moved from farm to farm in our wagon. Got milk, potatoes and cabbage for our services. Everything we needed. Now all the farms are burnt to the ground! How are we supposed to live? Six brass buttons buy a bag of flour, that's all I know!

BRAND: I don't want to hear your excuses! Just be quiet!

ANNA: Never ever a locket or keepsake. Never anything a woman gave them, and that's the truth. Only buttons... and buckles...pocket watches...and sometimes a few old boots. (*Sentimentally. Slightly tearful.*) And at least there's someone to close their eyes and fold their hands. And say a few kind words. Poor things. Hardly more than children, most of them.

BRAND: You think you're very clever! Well, I'm here to keep an eye on you.

ANNA: (*Suddenly pleading.*) Please don't think so badly of me. It's for my poor daughter. Really it is. She is so sick and weak and thin. Well... (*Pointing at ANNIE.*) ...you can see for yourself. Just look at her.

BRAND: (*With sudden violence.*) Be quiet, you vulture!

GENERAL: (*Suddenly opening his eyes wide.*) Adjutant... Adjutant...is that you?

BRAND: (*Suddenly very respectful.*) Yes General. (*Goes to him.*) Here I am. Adjutant Brand reporting. I have to speak to you, General. The men...

GENERAL: I had to send a party to look for you! Where have you been?

ANNA: He's a little delirious. It's the fever. He's doesn't know what he is saying.

GENERAL: (*Peering at ANNA.*) And who is that woman? We're going into battle and there's a woman here!

BRAND: (*Diplomatically.*) We're not going into battle right now, General

GENERAL: (*Violently.*) As I said, at first light we attack! Are you questioning my decision? (*Shouts.*) I'll have you shot for treason, as God is my witness! I'll have you shot! (*He sits up.*) Deserter! Traitor!

ANNA: (*Goes to him. Pushes him back onto the pillows.*) There there…don't get so excited. It's not good for you.

GENERAL: Take your hands off me! Who is this woman? Who is she? (*Grabs BRAND's arm. Hoarsely.*) When I give the first signal, we attack. Do you understand?

BRAND: Yes.

GENERAL: Have they dug the trenches wide and deep?

BRAND: Yes, General.

GENERAL: We'll drive them back! Shoot to kill! Did you tell them that?

BRAND: Yes, General.

GENERAL: Outnumbered…the plan… (*Suddenly struggles up and falls out of bed. He is quite naked. Shouting.*) Men!! When the sun… Ready! We're fighting for…our fatherland!

BRAND: Careful, General… (*Tries to lift him.*)

GENERAL: (*Resists. Sings loudly and tunelessly.*) 'Our fatherland…our fatherland…together…we must…stand …our…' (*Collapses and mutters.*)

ANNA: Look, he's wet himself again. (*Sighs.*) I've turned the straw so many times. Get him back into bed! Cover him up! There's a young innocent girl here!

(*BRAND gets the GENERAL onto the bed and puts the blanket over him.*)

BRAND: (*To ANNA.*) Why is he still like this? How can I talk to him if he's like this?

ANNA: (*Casually.*) Nature must take its course.

BRAND: (*Angrily.*) I was a fool to trust you. You're probably a fraud *and* a thief.

ANNA: (*Hissing.*) I'm only doing this because you begged me to! Do you think I want to be here? In this dank and stinking place?

GENERAL: (*Weak and confused.*) Who is that woman? Who is she? (*Suddenly groans with pain.*)

(*ANNA notices that ANNIE is sagging in the chair asleep.*)

ANNA: (*Rapidly moving towards her.*) My girl, you're falling asleep.

GENERAL: (*Pathetic. Whining.*) I'm dying…I'm dying.

ANNA: (*To ANNIE.*) You mustn't fall asleep. 'I must not fall asleep.' Say that over and over again. (*Puts on the harness.*)

I'll have to strap you in. I'm afraid it won't make a very
good impression.

GENERAL: (*Whining.*) Why don't you just shoot me. Get a
gun and shoot me. (*Whimpers.*)

ANNA: (*To ANNIE.*) I want to hear you say it!

ANNIE: I must not fall asleep.

ANNA: (*To ANNIE.*) Look at me and lift your head.

GENERAL: (*Suddenly fearful.*) Where am I?

ANNIE: Yes, mother.

GENERAL: I don't know this place.

BRAND: It's the shed on your farm, General. We've tried to
make it…comfortable.

GENERAL: Why aren't I at home in my bed?

BRAND: Your house has been burnt down General.

GENERAL: (*Looks around.*) And the cows? Where are the
cows?

BRAND: Been shot, General.

ANNA: (*Approaching with a bowl.*) Don't upset yourself about
these things.

GENERAL: And what is this woman doing here? I want my
wife. (*Like a child.*) I want my wife.

ANNIE: I must not fall asleep.

ANNA: Your wife is not here. (*To BRAND.*) Lift him up a little.
I want to feed him some of this.

BRAND: All the men can think about, General, are their
wives and children. (*Lifts the GENERAL up against the
pillows.*)

ANNA: I'm going to give you something to make you strong
again.

GENERAL: I don't want it. Leave me alone! Go away!

BRAND: The men have reached the end of their strength,
General.

ANNA: It will make you better General.

GENERAL: (*Suddenly whines.*) I don't want to die here. Die in
a cowshed like an animal.

ANNA: Well then open your mouth and have this.

(*The GENERAL opens his mouth. ANNA feeds him. He takes
a few spoons and then turns his head away.*)

147

BRAND: It's not easy for them, General.

GENERAL: (*Tearful.*) Dying...like an animal.

ANNIE: I must not fall asleep.

BRAND: Hungry and exhausted.

(*BRAND turns away. He seems deeply affected. He wipes his eyes with the back of his hand.*)

GENERAL: (*Weakly.*) I'll never...sit...on a horse...again. Never...again. (*He mutters a little and then his eyes close and he starts breathing heavily.*)

BRAND: They want to go home, General. If you're not there, how can I stop them? What can I tell them? They want to go back to what's left of their farms.

(*The deep monotonous breathing continues and underscores the action for much of the play unless otherwise indicated in the text.*)

(*Turning on ANNA.*) He is not getting any better! Just look at him!

ANNA: I'm doing everything I can. I didn't say I could work miracles, did I?

BRAND: If he dies, I'll kill you! Do you hear that!

ANNIE: I must stay awake.

BRAND: (*Agitated and confused.*) Why does she keep saying that? (*Passes his hand over his eyes.*) Over and over again. (*Notices the harness.*) And what is that?

ANNA: (*Patiently as if explaining to a child.*) It makes her sit up straight. Helps to keep her awake. She's so pale and weak. If she falls asleep now it would be such a deep sleep that no one would be able to wake her up again. (*Moves towards the GENERAL.*)

BRAND: (*Deeply perplexed.*) But is that true?

ANNA: Oh yes. (*Kneels next to the GENERAL, turns her head to the side and puts her head on his chest.*)

BRAND: What are you doing? Get away from him!

ANNA: (*Patiently. Getting up again.*) I'm just listening to his heart. It's beating strongly but it's very fast. (*Indicates ANNIE.*) Just look at her now. So pale and weak. How will I possibly keep her awake? (*Sudden cry of anguish.*) I'll lose her forever if she falls asleep!

BRAND: Is there nothing we can do? Surely we can't just stand by...

ANNA: While she slips away. Yes...yes...it's kind of you to be concerned.

BRAND: If she needs food, I can go out and find something.

ANNA: No thank you. What she needs is too difficult to find. She's not like you. Never has been. Not since she was born. (*Sighs.*) You wouldn't understand if I told you.

ANNIE: (*Weakly.*) I mustn't...fall...asleep.

BRAND: (*Very distressed.*) But is there nothing I can do?

ANNA: Well... (*Brightens.*) ...as a matter of fact there is... If you told her a story, then she'll stay awake. And I can rest for a little while.

BRAND: I don't know any stories.

ANNA: Oh, anything that's interesting. (*To ANNIE.*) The Adjutant wants to tell you something. Isn't that nice of him? (*To BRAND.*) Sit here. (*Indicates the bench at the table.*) The closer you are the better. I'll go over there in the corner. I need to rest. (*Suddenly sounding old and frail.*) This time of the night I feel so old and weary. (*Suddenly catches sight of BRAND. She gives a cry.*)

BRAND: (*Alarmed.*) What is it?

ANNA: Seeing you from the side like that...lit by the candle flame...as if it...reminded me of something. (*Rapidly shaking her head.*) I must be tired. Well go on. Say something my girl. Show that you're thankful.

ANNIE: Thank you.

BRAND: (*Clears his throat.*) The last time...we met the enemy...they weren't expecting us...

ANNA: (*Shrieks.*) No, not that! She doesn't want to hear about that! That makes her very sleepy. Tell her about your family. That will really please her. Do you have brothers and sisters?

BRAND: I had two brothers. But...both have been killed in the war.

ANNA: What a shame. And were you the eldest?

BRAND: No. The youngest.

ANNA: (*Suddenly excited.*) Do you hear that, my girl? The youngest of three! (*Sits down on the straw.*) Oh, my poor bones. How they ache. (*Yawns and then closes her eyes.*) (*Short silence.*)

BRAND: (*Shyly.*) Is there anything you want to hear about? I...don't really know what to tell you. I can't remember very much...before the war... What...happened before the war... It seems...too long ago. Feels as if the war...has been going on forever.

ANNIE: The light. Tell me about that.

BRAND: The light?

ANNIE: Mother won't tell me. She says the less I know about it the less I'll fret. Please tell me.

BRAND: The...light?

ANNIE: Yes. In the daytime the flap of the wagon must be closed very tightly. Not to let anything in. Sometimes we go outside just before the sun rises. Then we can see what the world looks like even if it's dim and gloomy. But I've never seen it shining. Never ever. Won't you tell me what it's like?

BRAND: Well...

ANNIE: Please.

BRAND: It's very bright.

ANNIE: And...it shines everywhere?

BRAND: Yes. And you can see everything. Birds...trees... and everything.

(*ANNIE gives a little gasp of pleasure. Short silence. They continue to look at each other.*)

(*Overcome. Searching for words.*) And when I signal to the men...I use a small mirror. I turn it to the sun...and it flashes.

(*He takes a small mirror out of his breast pocket and holds it up to the candle. He turns the mirror and flashes the reflection from the flame onto her face. She gasps with delight.*)

ANNA: (*Yawns loudly.*) Just to close my poor eyes for a little while. It's made me so happy I could cry. Forty winks can make such a difference. I'm quite refreshed. (*Gets up quickly and moves towards ANNIE.*) Well, let's look at you. My my,

you seem to have perked up quite a bit. You've been very
helpful Adjutant. How can I ever thank you?

BRAND: (*Still looking at ANNIE.*) It's my pleasure...

ANNA: What did you say?

BRAND: (*Repeating the words slowly.*) It's...my...pleasure.

ANNIE: Why did you speak in that way?

BRAND: I'm sorry if I...

ANNA: (*Repeating the phrase to herself.*) It's my pleasure...
(*Presses her fingertips to her forehead.*) Echoes...echoes...
(*Moans.*) It's as if...as if...I've heard it before. (*Shakes her
head.*) But I mustn't imagine things.

ANNIE: What is it mother?

ANNA: Oh I'm just imagining things. It's giving me a
headache. (*Holds up a finger urgently.*) Ssh. Ssh. Do you hear
that?

BRAND: (*Suspiciously.*) I don't hear anything.

ANNA: Yes. (*Listens.*) It's my horse. Pawing the ground. Why
is it suddenly so restless? Maybe there's someone out there!

BRAND: (*Picks up his gun.*) I'll have to go outside and see.

ANNA: I'll go with you.

BRAND: No. I have to go alone. I can't take a woman into
danger.

ANNA: I can see in the dark, and that can be very helpful. If
you don't believe me (*Indicates ANNIE.*) you can ask her.

BRAND: Well come along if you want to. But close the door
behind you. We don't want any light to show. (*To ANNIE.
Gently.*) Don't be afraid. (*Little laugh.*) I shoot very straight.

ANNA: Yes, yes my girl. Stay here quietly. We're just going to
see and then we'll be back. You stay here safely and don't
make a sound.

ANNIE: Please...don't leave me alone.

BRAND: We'll be back soon.

ANNA: Yes...yes.

ANNIE. Please...

BRAND: (*Tenderly.*) Nothing will happen to you. I give you my
word.

ANNIE: But what...if you get hurt?

ANNA: (*To BRAND.*) Come you. Don't just stand there.

(*They exit and close the door behind them. Complete silence except for the GENERAL's deep, heavy breathing. ANNIE sits motionless. After a time she gets up slowly and starts moving very tentatively towards the door. She almost reaches the door when she falls gently to the ground. Short silence. The door opens and ANNA enters.*)

BRAND: (*Voice from outside.*) Are you sure?

ANNA: (*Calling back to him.*) Of course I'm sure. I saw it vanishing into the shadows. Poor thing. The thinnest jackal I've ever seen. (*Catches sight of ANNIE lying on the floor and rushes towards her. To BRAND.*) Help me! Help! (*To ANNIE.*) You're not asleep? Open you eyes!

(*BRAND enters quickly and moves towards ANNIE.*)

BRAND: What's happened?

ANNA: (*Crooning.*) My poor little girl. Your hands are like ice. (*Blows into her hands. To BRAND.*) Pick her up and take her to the stove! Come on!

(*BRAND picks ANNIE up and carries her to the stove.*)

Put her down on the chair.

(*BRAND puts her carefully in the armchair.*)

Now go and fetch my shawl in the wagon! And hurry up! (*BRAND exits rapidly.*)

(*Whispers harshly into ANNIE's ear.*) We must work quickly my girl. I have to put aside my stupid fancies and do what must be done. And you must help me. You must! You must do everything you can. You must use all your strength for this. Say: 'Yes mother.'

ANNIE: (*Weakly.*) Yes, mother.

ANNA: Good girl.

(*BRAND enters with the shawl.*)

(*To BRAND.*) About time. (*Takes the shawl and puts it around ANNIE's shoulders.*) That should make her feel much warmer.

BRAND: Is there anything else I can do?

ANNA: I must say...she's already looking a little better. (*Moves to the table. Picks up the honey.*) First I'll feed her a spoonful of honey. (*Moves back to ANNIE. Dips her finger in the honey.*) Open your mouth my girl.

(*ANNIE opens her mouth. ANNA rubs her finger over ANNIE's lips and ANNIE passes her tongue over her lips.*)
That should keep you going for a while. (*To BRAND.*)
I want you to look after her. I have to go out for a little while. (*Puts the honey on the table.*)

BRAND: (*Panic stricken.*) But where are you going? Surely you shouldn't leave her like this?

ANNA: I've noticed that the moon is out. Nice and big and bright. Now I can see where the roots are. I need to get some more. I must make another poultice for his wound. (*To ANNIE.*) Are you feeling warmer now my girl? (*Sighs.*) Oh there's so little wood. We can only put in one log at a time and it hardly gives off any warmth. (*To BRAND.*) Watch her carefully. She mustn't shiver. That's very bad for her. But if she does you must hold her close. Sometimes when it's very cold I have to hold her all night. To give her all my warmth. (*To ANNIE.*) Chin up my girl I'll see you in a while. (*Moves towards the door.*)

BRAND: (*To ANNIE.*) You could put on my jacket if you like. It's nearly dry.

ANNA: (*Stopping at the door. To BRAND.*) No no! It would be too heavy for her. Her bones are very delicate. And remember…if you must hold her…you must do it very gently. You don't want to hurt her. (*Exits.*)
(*Silence. BRAND looks ill at ease. ANNIE looks down at her hands but from time to time she peers at him from under her lashes. She lifts her head and looks at him. He feels her watching him. He turns around and looks at her. A short electric look passes between them. They both look away.*)

ANNIE: (*Looking down at her hands. Quite simply.*) I was so afraid that something would happen to you out there. So afraid…that it made my bones ache.

BRAND: (*Moved and hardly believing what he hears.*) Really?

ANNIE: Yes.
(*He moves towards her and sits shyly on the chair near her. Silence. BRAND lifts the stove plate and stokes the fire. He throws down the poker. Short silence.*)

BRAND: It was nothing. Just a jackal.

ANNIE: (*Gives a gentle little laugh and shakes her head.*)
Strange…it's almost as if I've never known anyone before.
Not even my mother. Before you. I thought I did. Yes.
But…it wasn't true. It wasn't… (*Closes her eyes.*)
(*Short silence. BRAND turns his head and looks at her. He sees
that her eyes are closed. He panics, then takes the honey and dips
his finger in. He passes his finger over her lips. She sighs and
licks off the honey. Then she opens her eyes.*)

ANNIE: (*Quietly.*) I know you.

BRAND: (*Quietly. Puzzled.*) I know you too. But…I've never
met you before.

ANNIE: I've been travelling in our wagon. Never stopping
for very long. Since I was small. I've been travelling
always. But…now I know why. All these years… travelling.
Years…and years. (*Looks up at him. Gentle, radiant smile.*)
Following tracks I couldn't see. Tracks… made by the
shadow of birds… By the wind blowing through the
grass…and the light of the stars. Sometimes I would
think…now what does that mean? It means something.
But what? When we were coming here…it was a tree. I
kept looking back at it. A tree in the moonlight. The way
it leaned to one side. It was telling me something. (*Little
laugh.*) Oh, things like that. From time to time I've seen
them and I wondered. But that was before. Before I saw
you. Before I knew you. (*Happily.*) Now I don't have to
wonder any more. Everything…was leading me here.
Where you could find me. I've been so far. So lost and
alone.
(*BRAND is motionless. He continues to look at her. He seems
dazed with perplexed wonder. ANNIE lifts her pale hand slowly
and puts it on his sleeve. She looks up at him with complete and
simple trust. BRAND catches his breath.*)

BRAND: (*Looking at her deeply.*) Your face…I never knew…
that anyone could have a face like yours. Your…face. (*Very
gently he puts his hand over hers.*) Your hand…is so small and
cold.

ANNIE: Why…are you trembling? (*Lifts her hand and presses it
against her chest.*) And your heart…is beating so fast…

(*Suddenly BRAND half-lifts ANNIE, as he presses her against him. ANNA appears noiselessly at the door and peers in. BRAND kisses ANNIE's hair and face. ANNA enters noisily. BRAND puts ANNIE back in the chair and turns away. He is very flustered.*)

ANNA: The birds are fluttering in the trees. At this time of night. It makes me uneasy. (*Moves towards ANNIE and puts her hand against ANNIE's cheek.*) So...I see you've been keeping her warm. That's so kind of you. (*Moves towards the table and puts down her bag.*) I found roots quite close by under the willow tree. (*Sighs.*) I've got mud under my nails and I'm completely filthy. But the roots are good and I'll boil them up. (*Goes back to ANNIE.*) Now let me look at you properly my girl. Ah! Not so pale any more. (*To BRAND.*) You've looked after her very well. You must thank the Adjutant for being so good to you my girl. Where are your manners?

ANNIE: (*Concealing a smile. Quietly.*) Thank you.
  (*Silence. BRAND gets up and moves about restlessly. He keeps looking at ANNIE and then looking away again. He goes to the GENERAL and looks at him. He seems very distressed. ANNA is standing very still and watching him. ANNIE sits motionless, looking down at her hands.*)

BRAND: I'm sorry...if you'll excuse me...I feel a little... I think I need some fresh air...yes...yes...some fresh air...
  (*Moves towards the door.*)

ANNA: Excuse me, Adjutant!
  (*BRAND stops at the door. Looks uncertain.*)
  Why don't you...put those boots on...just for now? You can take them off when you get back. (*Picks up the boots.*) Come now. It's dark and you won't be able to see. Many sharp stones and bones from the dead animals. Bones are dirty and very dangerous. If they stick into your feet... you might die. Even I couldn't save you. And what good would that do? (*Holds out the boots.*) Take them. Just for now. (*BRAND hesitates, then takes the boots. He takes off his shoes. ANNA grabs them and puts them near the stove. He hastily pulls on the boots and leaves.*)

(*Calling after him.*) Be careful out there! It's very wet and slippery! (*Silence as she goes to the door and looks out.*) I can't see him. He must be walking very fast. (*Gives a strange laugh.*) Maybe he's running. (*Closes the door and moves towards ANNIE.*) Well my girl, I'm very pleased with you. Very pleased. You've obviously done precisely what I've told you to. But I must say… (*Looking towards the door.*) it's gone even better than I expected. He's properly bewildered!

GENERAL: (*In his sleep.*) Shoot them all! Shoot them! Deserters!

ANNA: Oh be quiet! I've had enough of you.

(*The GENERAL mutters incoherently under his breath. This muttering continues until otherwise indicated.*)

Tell me about it my girl. You know I always want to hear everything.

ANNIE: Why did he leave so suddenly?

ANNA: You know it's happened before. Don't you remember? It almost always happens. They're completely overcome and they don't know what to do. (*Gives a strange laugh.*)

ANNIE: (*Very nervously.*) But what if he never comes back?

(*The GENERAL stops muttering.*)

ANNA: He'll come back. They always do.

ANNIE: Maybe he's taken his horse and gone away for ever.

ANNA: I'm sure it's still here. We would have heard.

ANNIE: (*Now very agitated.*) Are you sure? Won't you go and see mother? Please go and see.

ANNA: What's the matter with you? All right, all right I'll go and see. (*Moves to the door opens it and peers out.*) There it still is.

(*ANNIE looks relieved.*)

(*Still looking out.*) Poor thing. Just skin and bone. I think it's sleeping. Must be funny, to sleep on your feet. That's what I always think. But we'll fatten it up. This really is a piece of luck. (*Closes the door and turns back to ANNIE.*) Well I hope you're satisfied. I don't know what's wrong with you. Is there something you're not telling me?

ANNIE: (*Shaking her head.*) No.

ANNA: You didn't change anything did you?

ANNIE: No I didn't.

ANNA: Did you say all the usual things?

(*ANNIE nods.*)

(*Chuckles.*) That's good. It always works. (*Continues to chuckle while ANNIE speaks her next line.*)

ANNIE: (*Repeating the line with wonder and delight. Speaking under her breath.*) 'I've never...seen a face...like yours.'

ANNA: (*Very suspiciously.*) What was that? I've never heard anything like that before? You're not supposed to make things up. Did you make things up? Come on. Spit it out.

ANNIE: No. Nothing.

ANNA: Look at me.

(*ANNIE looks at ANNA.*)

I know those eyes. You're hiding something aren't you? (*ANNIE shakes her head vehemently. She continues to shake her head as ANNA speaks.*)

It won't do my girl. It won't do for you to get all kinds of funny notions in your head. Maybe you think that he is the one. He's just a weak man like all the others, weak believe me.

(*ANNIE stops shaking her head and looks down at her hands.*)

Well, if you fancy him a little, it's not such a bad thing. Quite nice to have a little flutter. Good for the circulation. But just don't take it seriously. That would be the death of you my girl. The death! But you don't look quite right. Something happened. Come on now. Tell me. You'll have to tell me in the end. You know that.

ANNIE: I was just thinking...

ANNA: Yes?

ANNIE: That he might be different.

ANNA: Ha!

ANNIE: Maybe...maybe he'll just start walking and walking and never come back.

ANNA: How can you say it like that? As if it makes you happy! You know what that would mean my girl? Don't you? It would be the end! (*Suddenly crying noisily.*) And I would lose you. What would I do then? What would I do then? (*Wipes her eyes.*) What am I crying for? He wants you. I could see that. Oh, he'll be back. (*Sniggers.*) He'll be back, he'll be back.

GENERAL: (*Muttering in his sleep.*) Death to the enemy… death…

ANNA: Just you wait and see my girl. And don't worry your pretty little head. Everything will be all right.

(*The GENERAL moans and then starts breathing heavily. He continues breathing heavily until otherwise indicated in the text.*)

And see what I found for him! A treat! (*Moves to the table and opens the bag.*) We need to feed him up a little. He looks so gaunt. Look! A dead bird! It's quite fresh. Even slightly warm. Must have been killed by the storm, poor thing. Pity, pity it's so small and thin. (*Goes to ANNIE and shows her the bird.*)

(*ANNIE turns her head away.*)

(*Moving back to the table.*) I'll have to scrape every morsel off the bone. (*Rummages in the bag.*) And I found a few wild onions for flavouring. But I have to pluck it first. I'm sure it will please him. (*Starts plucking the bird with her back to ANNIE.*)

(*ANNIE sees BRAND's hat lying near the chair. She bends over and picks it up.*)

Quite tough to get the feathers off. (*Continues to pluck while she starts humming.*)

(*ANNIE cradles the hat in her lap. She touches the brim very softly with her fingers.*)

It's so bony that I can't quite get a hold on it. (*As she continues to pluck she starts singing.*)

(*While ANNA sings the song, in a strangely high and quavering voice, interspersed by sound of irritation as she struggles to remove the feathers, ANNIE continues to cradle the hat. After the first few lines, she lifts up the hat and looks into its crown as if she is seeing deep into another world. Towards the end of the song the lights fade very slowly to black.*)

ANNA's song:

He has a horse, a big black horse.
And he's taking us away.
He has a horse, a big black horse.
And he's taking us away.
Taking us to a far off land,
Where the night is light as day.
He has a horse, a big black horse.
And he's taking us away.
He has a horse, a big black horse.
And he's taking us away.
He has a horse, a big black horse.
And he's taking us away.
Taking us to a far off land,
Where the night is light as day.
He has a horse, a big black horse.
And he's taking us away.

ACT TWO

Lights slowly up. ANNIE is sitting motionless on a chair near the fire. She is very pale. After a few moments the door is pushed open and BRAND enters.

ANNIE: Is that you?

BRAND: Yes. (*He stays near the door.*)

ANNIE: I thought you'd never come back. I was so afraid. I've been ringing and ringing my hands. Look. (*Holds up her hands.*) I've broken the skin.

BRAND: (*Roughly.*) Where is your mother?

ANNIE: I sent her to go and look for you. I thought something might have happened.

BRAND: And why did you think that?

ANNIE: It's been hours and hours. Why do you keep standing near the door?
(*Silence. BRAND comes a little closer but doesn't look at her.*)
Why won't you look at me?

BRAND: I… I've… (*Passes his hand over his eyes.*) I've just come…to say goodbye. I have to get back to my men. They need me you see. They're so tired and worn out. Hungry and cold. If I leave them too long they disappear. So many deserters now. I have to talk to them and give them hope. To keep close to them and to tell them. Where there's life there's hope that's what I'll tell them.

ANNIE: Yes. (*Nods a few times. Short silence.*) You must go. (*Suddenly urgent.*) You must go now.

BRAND: Yes. I don't want to… But I have my duty. (*As if convincing himself.*) I have my duty. (*Short silence.*) Tell your mother that someone will fetch the General in a few days if he is better. Then you can be on your way. (*Puts on his hat.*)

ANNIE: Yes. (*Quietly.*) You must go. Before my mother comes back.

BRAND: (*Takes the gun and slings it over his shoulder. Moves to the door. Short silence. Turns at the door.*) And after this…where will you go?

ANNIE: (*Quietly.*) I don't know.

BRAND: I'm sure we'll meet again. After all this is over.

ANNIE: (*Gently.*) I don't think so.

BRAND: We might.

(*ANNIE shakes her head.*)

So... I'll never see you again.

ANNIE: No. (*Looks down at her hands.*)

BRAND: Never.

(*ANNIE and BRAND look at each other.*)

(*Quietly. Shakes his head.*) I don't want to think about that.

(*Short silence. Opens the door. Looks back.*) I won't forget you.

ANNIE: (*Not looking at him.*) And I won't forget you.

(*Short silence.*)

BRAND: I'll always think about you.

ANNIE: And I'll think about you. No matter where I go.

BRAND: When I close my eyes...I'll see your face.

ANNIE: Will you? Are you sure?

BRAND: Yes.

ANNIE: And I'll see yours. When I close mine.

(*Short silence.*)

And I'll hear your voice when it's quiet at night.

BRAND: (*Sadly and quietly.*) And what will I be saying?

ANNIE: (*Wan little smile.*) I don't know.

BRAND: Well I must go now. Goodbye Annie. Goodbye.

(*BRAND exits and closes the door softly behind him. ANNIE sits very still. After a few moments the door opens and BRAND appears again. ANNIE starts shivering.*)

I'm sorry but I almost forgot. (*Moves towards ANNIE.*) I must take these boots off and leave them behind. The shoes are broken but at least they're mine. (*He crouches down to undo the laces.*)

(*ANNIE makes a small sound. BRAND looks up, then gets up and moves towards her.*)

BRAND: You're shivering.

ANNIE: It's nothing.

BRAND: (*Taking her hands.*) You're cold. So cold.

ANNIE: Go now. (*Pulling her hands away.*) Go.

BRAND: (*Touches her face.*) And your face is cold.

ANNIE: The fire has gone out.

BRAND: How can I go if you're so cold. I can see you
shivering. (*Unslings his gun.*) You know what your mother
told me. I have to hold you close to make you warm. (*He
lifts her out of the chair and holds her close to him. He gives
a soft moan. Brokenly.*) I was walking…walking. I didn't
even know where I was going. Or what was happening
to me. (*Short silence. Buries his face in her hair. Quietly.*) I've
been saying over and over. 'They need me. My men. My
General. My country. We've sacrificed everything. For
victory.' (*Holds her very closely.*) But it makes no difference.
I know that if I can't be with you… Anywhere else…is a
strange country.
(*ANNIE cries quietly.*)
Why are you crying?

ANNIE: Because it's terrible. (*Looks up at him.*) Because I'm
happy.
(*BRAND takes her face in his hands. Then he kisses her very softly
and lingeringly. ANNA opens the door very quietly. She watches
as BRAND continues to kiss ANNIE now with a desperate and
growing passion. Then ANNA enters noisily. ANNIE sits down
and BRAND turns away.*)

ANNA: Well here you are! I've been searching high and low!
My silly girl. You never believe me. Here he is and safe
and sound. I've found a few pieces of wood. (*Moves towards
the fire.*) I hope the fire isn't quite dead. (*Opens the top plate.*)
At least there's a little glow. (*She puts a log on and blows into
the fire.*) The poor girl was terribly worried. (*Replaces the
plate of the stove. Wipes her hands on her dress.*) Been keeping
her warm have you?
(*Makes a sign to BRAND suggesting that she wants to speak to
him alone. He helps ANNIE back in the chair and then follows
ANNA.*)
Look what I've found. (*Puts her hand in her apron pocket and
takes out a locket.*) I saw it shining. Hanging from a branch.

BRAND: What is it?

ANNA: It's a locket. Now let me see what it says on the back.
(*Squints to see.*) 'To my dearest wife from her devoted
husband.' And a date. (*Opens the locket.*) And look…there's

a picture inside. Nice man with a beard. (*Surprised.*) I think
it is the General. But he must have been much younger.
Pure gold. And such a lovely, delicate chain.

BRAND: Give it to me. It must have belonged to his wife.

ANNE: (*Ominously.*) What was it doing…hanging from a tree?
No, I'd rather not think about that. (*Confidentially.*) Why
don't you give it to Annie? She's never had anything so
fine.

BRAND: Didn't I tell you! It belongs to the General's wife!
Give it here at once.

ANNA: Oh, she won't be needing it any more where she's
gone. (*Pleadingly.*) Oh come now. Just think how pretty
she'll look with this…glowing against her skin. Poor little
thing. She'll be so grateful. Don't you want to make her
happy?

BRAND: I don't know… It doesn't seem right.

ANNA: What are you waiting for? Go on! And she'll give you
such a lovely smile.

BRAND: Well…I suppose…

ANNA: But first we have to take the picture out. (*Takes out the
picture and throws it on the ground.*)

BRAND: Don't do that. Have some respect. (*Retrieves the
picture and puts it in his breast pocket.*)

ANNA: What she would really like… (*Claps her hands together.*)
is some of your hair in the locket. Yes! That would really
please her. And what luck. I always carry a small pair of
scissors in my pocket. (*Takes a small pair of scissors out of her
pocket.*) Here. (*Goes to BRAND and tries to get some of his hair.*)

BRAND: Stay away from me.

ANNA: But surely it's not too much to ask when it will make
her so very happy. She'll always keep it. She'll be buried
with it. And I'll just cut the smallest piece. You won't even
notice.

BRAND: Oh well…

ANNA: Just keep still. (*Cuts a bit of hair. Her hand slips.*) I'm so
sorry!

BRAND: That hurt! (*Touches his hair then looks at his finger.*)
You've drawn blood, you stupid woman!

ANNA: I must really apologise very deeply. I hardly know what to say. I've only tried to please my Annie. Please don't be angry.

(*BRAND grumbles. ANNA puts the hair in the locket.*)

(*Loudly, to ANNIE.*) The Adjutant has a present for you! Isn't that nice of him? He's a really kind man. Show her what it is. Close your eyes my girl. No peeping.

(*BRAND goes towards the GENERAL. He seems confused and undecided.*)

Now you can open!

(*ANNIE opens her eyes.*)

ANNIE: Where is it?

(*BRAND opens his palm and shows her the locket.*)

Is it really for me?

BRAND: Yes.

ANNIE: How it shines. I've never seen anything so shiny.

ANNA: And it can open.

ANNIE: What's inside? (*Struggles to open it.*)

ANNA: Tell her. (*Takes the gun and hangs it back on the hook.*)

BRAND: Some of…my hair.

ANNIE: Your hair? (*With wonder and delight.*) Your…hair is…in here?

BRAND: Yes.

(*ANNIE sighs with pleasure. She holds the locket between her hands as if to warm it. She opens her hands and looks at it again. Looks up at BRAND.*)

ANNIE: Will you put it on for me? (*Gives it to him.*)

(*BRAND goes behind her and fastens the locket behind her neck while she lifts up her hair. ANNA watches silently and solemnly.*)

ANNA: (*After a silence.*) There! Pretty as a picture. Don't you agree Adjutant?

BRAND: Very very pretty.

ANNIE: (*Radiant. Looks up at him.*) Thank you.

ANNA: (*Jabs him with her elbow.*) Why don't you kiss her at least? But only on her cheek.

(*BRAND bends down formally and kisses ANNIE on her cheek.*)

GENERAL: (*Opening his eyes. Very agitated.*) All around us!
A wall of fire! Black smoke! Dark black smoke! Hold the
horses! Keep them calm! The heat! Hot!

ANNA: (*Moves towards him.*) There…there. It's just a dream.
(*The GENERAL murmurs and his eyes close very slowly.*)
(*Feeling his head.*) He's very very feverish. I can only hope
that the poultice is doing its work.

BRAND: He's dreaming about the last battle. It was on a hill.
We were waiting for them.

GENERAL: (*Muttering.*) Fire…fire.

BRAND: The wind turned. The General noticed it first. It
turned suddenly. You know how it is. Both of us were
waving and shouting. Warning the men to get out. They
didn't expect that. Many of them…were burned that day.

ANNA: Poor things. (*Sighs. Goes to the table and pours water from
the jug into the bowl.*)

BRAND: (*Going to ANNIE. Tenderly.*) How are you feeling?

ANNIE: Tired and happy. A little sleepy…

BRAND: But you mustn't sleep. You know what your mother
says.

ANNA: I'm completely covered in dirt! Mud and slime and
who knows what else! I can even smell dung. Please look
away Adjutant, I have to take off my dress. You must
forgive me, but modesty is a luxury I can't afford.

ANNIE: (*Smiling at BRAND.*) I won't sleep. Because then I
have to close my eyes. I don't want to do that, because I
want to look at you. Look and look.

BRAND: (*Smiles.*) Me too.
(*They laugh quietly together.*)

ANNA: (*Washing herself voluptuously.*) The water is cold.
(*Shivers.*) And there is a sharp wind. Oh, I must have left
the door open. Close it, won't you Adjutant? I'm half
naked and I'll catch a cold.
(*BRAND goes to the door and looks out.*)
A storm is brewing up again. (*Continues to wash. As she
washes she starts humming a strange, discordant melody.*) Close
the door will you?
(*The GENERAL moans softly and starts breathing deeply as
before. BRAND closes the door and turns around slowly.*)

BRAND: My men…are out there. All alone… But I don't want to leave. I really don't. It's only that…

ANNIE: (*Turns her head away. To her mother with a catch in her voice.*) The Adjutant has to go away mother.

BRAND: (*Softly.*) But I don't want to. I don't. (*Confused.*) What must I do?

ANNIE: (*Still to her mother.*) He has to go. He must go now.

BRAND: (*Averting his eyes.*) It's…my duty, you see. I'm…so sorry. (*Almost relieved.*) Yes. It's my duty!

ANNA: It is true Adjutant? Must you leave?

BRAND: It's only…for a little while…I promise I'll be back.

ANNA: Well, if you have to go…then there's nothing to be done.

BRAND: Well then…I only need to put on my shoes. (*He goes over to the fire and crouches down to untie the laces of the boots.*)

ANNA: As soon as he's better (*Indicates the GENERAL.*) we'll have to go. And even if he's not…we can't stay here much longer. This place is very unhealthy.

BRAND: (*To ANNIE.*) Where will you go when you leave here?

ANNA: I don't know. We travel all the time. (*Yawns.*) Mostly at night. It's difficult to see where we are. Sometimes it all seems the same to me.

BRAND: (*To ANNIE.*) And the day? Where are you then?

ANNA: (*Disinterestedly.*) We hide. Caves or ravines or dry river beds. But we stay in the wagon because bright light hurts us. (*Sighs.*) That feels much better. I'm going to put on a nice clean dress.

BRAND: (*To ANNIE.*) So…where will I find you?

ANNA: (*Going over to the trunk and rummaging.*) I really can't say.

BRAND: (*Getting up. To ANNIE.*) But what if I never find you again?

ANNIE: (*Quite simply.*) It will give me pain. (*Touches her heart.*) Like a bruise that never goes away.

BRAND: (*Passes his hand over his eyes.*) I must know where you are. Every day. Every minute.

ANNIE: You must go. Now.

BRAND: I must always know where to find you.
(*Short silence.*)
ANNIE: (*Closes her eyes.*) Yes.
(*BRAND seems distressed and is thinking deeply. ANNA picks up the bowl, carries it to the door, opens the door and throws the water out. The sound of a horse neighing.*)
ANNA: I frightened the poor thing. (*Gives a laugh. Moves to the table to put the bowl down.*)
BRAND: (*Suddenly hopeful.*) But you can stay here and wait for me. I'll come every few days to see you.
ANNIE: (*Happy.*) Will you? Will you? (*Suddenly sad.*) I don't know what my mother will say. I don't think she'll want to.
BRAND: Then I'll talk to your mother.
ANNIE: You will?
BRAND: Yes, I'll talk to her.
ANNA: (*Takes a small comb out of her pocket and starts combing her long hair.*) What are you whispering about? If I didn't know any better I would think you're up to something. (*She combs her hair and she starts humming again. This time very loudly.*)
BRAND: (*Moves towards ANNA.*) I have to talk to you.
(*ANNA pretends not to hear him. She continues to hum and comb her hair.*)
I have to talk to you!
ANNA: What were you saying?
BRAND: I said that I want to talk to you.
ANNA: I really have such a lot to do and anyway, weren't you just leaving?
BRAND: But I must speak to you first. (*Suddenly emphatic.*) I want to talk to you now!
ANNA: Well! I can see that you're an Adjutant! So what is it that you want to say?
BRAND: I want to ask if you will stay here...for just a little longer.
ANNA: And why would we want to do that? In this dank place? This place will be the death of us. And we can only survive if we keep moving.
BRAND: Please.

ANNA: We have to do what we have to do. And that's the way it is.

BRAND: Won't you listen to me!

ANNA: Goodness me. I'm not one of your men to be ordered about. How dare you speak like that to me!

BRAND: I'm sorry...please...I'm sorry...just listen. If you stay here...I'll look after you. I'll bring you food when I get back. And wood.

ANNA: Food and wood? Where will you find that?

BRAND: I'll hunt.

ANNA: Hunt? (*She laughs sarcastically.*)

BRAND: I'll do anything. I'll even steal, if I have to.

ANNA: Excuse me? What did you say? And you called me a thief!

BRAND: (*Desperately.*) It doesn't matter any more! I don't care!

ANNA: And why would you want to do that? And why should I believe you? (*As if something suddenly dawns on her.*) Oh...I see...now I understand. Do you...fancy my daughter? It must be that. Well that makes all the difference. In that case we have many things to talk about. (*Confidentially.*) But I don't want her to hear. That wouldn't be proper. You'll have to carry her back to the wagon for a while. She's quite comfortable there. (*Loudly to ANNIE.*) My girl, the Adjutant wants to speak to me! And that's the right and proper thing to do. (*To BRAND. Coyly.*) Oh look, I think she's blushing. The Adjutant will carry you and see that you're quite warm. Go on! Pick her up! And when you get to the wagon wrap her snugly in the skins. (*Takes the skins off the GENERAL and wraps them around ANNIE. The GENERAL is left under a very thin, soiled cover.*)
(*BRAND picks her up very gently. She puts her arms around his neck.*)
Like a feather isn't she? Now remember my girl you mustn't fall asleep. To keep awake you must count the stars. And if the clouds come back you must listen to the wind.

ANNIE: Yes mother.

(*BRAND carries her out.*)

ANNA: (*Talking to herself.*) It's going well…but I don't feel
    right. There is something…I can feel it in my bones. And
    I have a humming in my ears…a tightness in my throat…
    (*Clasps her hands together.*) Now pull yourself together.
    Stop imagining things. These funny feelings don't mean
    anything. Tomorrow they'll be gone.
    (*ANNA moves quickly to the trunk. Looks inside. She takes out
    a dress, puts it on. It is a close-fitting dark red dress with a low
    neck. This changes her appearance dramatically. She suddenly
    looks younger and the white flesh of her swelling breasts make
    her seem almost alluring. She twists her hair up loosely. A few
    tendrils stray into her neck. There is a perceptible change in her
    bearing. She seems taller and more shapely.*
    *BRAND enters. He stops in the doorway and looks a little
    confused, almost as if he doesn't recognise ANNA.*)
    Is she quite snug?

BRAND: Well… I covered her up.

ANNA: Oh, I'm sorry to ask you… I hope you don't mind…
    Annie always does it for me, but she's not here. Would you
    button me up? I hope you don't find it an immodest thing
    to ask. But I can't reach all the way to the back. I would be
    very grateful.

BRAND: Well…
    (*ANNA moves to him, turns her back and waits. Silence while
    BRAND fumbles and buttons ANNA's dress.*)

ANNA: Thank you so much. It's a good thing we're alone isn't
    it?

BRAND: (*Uncomfortably.*) Yes.

ANNA: (*Moving to the bench. She sits down and pats the space next
    to her.*) Come and sit here next to me. Come on. I promise
    I won't bite.
    (*BRAND continues to stand. He looks uncomfortable.*)
    (*Gasps.*) What a huge shadow you have Adjutant. I feel as
    if I might slip right into it and vanish completely. (*Gives a
    coquettish laugh. Looks up at him. Her face crumples. She puts
    her hand into her cleavage and takes out a handkerchief. She dabs
    her eyes.*) I'm sorry…but I'm so deeply moved. So deeply.

I can see that you really care about my Annie. She's a
lucky girl. But I'm sure she knows it. I'm so sorry…I'm
a bit overcome. (*Blows her nose loudly, then crumples up the
handkerchief and puts it back in her cleavage.*) She's a good
girl. Sweet natured. And a kind heart. When she's stronger
she'll fill out a little. She'll be softer. And fuller. (*Sly smile.*) I
know what a man likes. And you won't have to be afraid of
crushing her. (*Sniggers.*) But she is weak now. So feeble, and
getting weaker all the time. Something will have to be done
if you don't want to lose her.

BRAND: (*Alarmed.*) Lose her?

ANNA: There is not much time. I have to be honest with you.
(*Sighs.*) Seeing that you're going to look after us… Going to
be…part of the family… It seems to me…that you should
know everything. The nature…of her condition.

BRAND: (*Distressed.*) She's not going to die, is she?

ANNA: Not if we…do what is necessary. Maybe…I shouldn't
be telling you this. I don't want to upset you. After all…
you have to go away…on important business.

BRAND: Please! You must tell me!

ANNA: You might be distressed.

BRAND: I don't care!

ANNA: Well, I suppose I have to. After all…it's a matter of
life and death.

BRAND: Is it that serious?

ANNA: It is. Yes. It is.

BRAND: Well, come on woman! What are you waiting for!

ANNA: Don't shout! Please. I have a headache starting
just behind my left eye. I'll tell you then. I'll tell you
everything. And if you care for my daughter…

BRAND: But I do!

ANNA: (*Holds up her hand to silence him. Looks at him piercingly.*)
I mean…really. Then you'll be able to help me.

BRAND: Of course I'll help. I'll do anything.

ANNA: (*Quietly.*) We'll see. You must sit over there. (*Points
to the chair at the stove.*) And you must be quiet. You must
listen from the beginning to the end. There is no other way.
And I'll put all the candles on the table. All the candles.

(*She continues to speak. She arranges the candles on the table.*) I
want you to see me. Sit down where I told you to!
(*BRAND sits.*)
I want you to see me very, very clearly. I want you to
see...all my suffering. In my eyes. In the lines in my
face. The grey in my hair. And my mouth. The way the
words come out of my mouth. Each...bitter word that I
have to spit out. (*She sits slowly on the chair behind the table.
The concentrated candlelight makes her face look garish and
deeply shadowed.*) I don't want to remember...I don't want
to. (*Groans and buries her face in her hands, lifting her head.
Fiercely.*) But I have to! (*She mutters to herself.*) Let me begin.
(*Moans and groans as if she is in pain. Takes a deep breath then
exhales very, very slowly. Her out-breath sounds like a long sigh.
She slumps forward onto the table. For a moment she seems almost
lifeless. When she starts speaking she is still lying with her head
on the table.*) The first time I saw him...he was holding a
cleft stick and looking for water. There was a big drought
and the farmer needed him. I watched him moving quietly.
Feeling the deep water flowing. His strong arms...and his
black eyes. I couldn't stop. I looked and looked. (*Lifts her
head, leans forward. Speaks urgently.*) I know what you're
feeling. Fire...moving under the skin. And nothing...is the
same. (*Sits back in the chair and stares into the candle flames.
Short silence.*) I asked...if I could come with him. And he
said yes. After that we were always together. He promised
but he was always restless. (*Sits forward, presses her hands
together and looks down.*) One morning...I woke up and he
was gone. I called him. I looked for him. Days. Nights. He
was gone. (*Looks up.*) Everything was black. Even when the
sun was shining. (*Looks into the flames. Pulls her finger through
the flames.*) Then one day...I knew I'd have a child. At first
I was happy. Because it was something of him. Something I
would always keep with me. And I felt so tenderly towards
the child. But then...the longing burnt in me again. The
sun came up, the sun went down. The wind, flowers grew
and the rain fell. But I only knew that I wanted him. From
the soles of my feet to the roots of my hair. Everything

seemed endless and empty because he wasn't there. Everything. Forever. (*She drops her head into her hands. Moves her head from side to side.*) But…I had something. Something to bargain with. And I started promising. I'll give up the child if I can find him again. I'll give up the only thing that was life to me. Anything. I kept repeating that over and over again. 'The child for him. The child for him.' I lit candles and burnt herbs every morning and every night. And slowly… I could feel the child…becoming quiet inside me. And then one night I could hear the child…go dead quiet. Sense it growing cold…as a stone. I became afraid. Maybe I'd made a mistake. I wept and hid my face under my hair. But then…suddenly…I heard his voice calling to me. Very quickly…I put on all my finery and went out to look for him. I found him sitting under a tree. He was tired and thirsty and half starved. He'd been walking…he told me…never stopping or sleeping. Looking for me. I was happy. I couldn't believe how happy I was. I helped him to the wagon. I wiped the dust off his face and kissed his eyes. I could feel the child quite still now. Not a flutter or a breath. But I didn't care, God help me. I didn't care. (*Leans forward. Urgently.*) You must know that I've been cursed for this! Oh yes! I never get any rest! Get any sleep! I have to keep my eyes open! To watch over her! It never ends! (*Short silence. She sits back in the chair.*) He slept for a while and then he woke. He told me…he loved a woman who didn't want him. He couldn't eat. He couldn't sleep. He could only think…of one thing. That's why he was looking for me. He said only I could help him. With my roots and herbs and secret spells. He pleaded with me. He blubbered and smeared his tears all over his face. Only then I remembered my child. Still now…still as death. Its life given up…for a faithless man. As I watched him…weak and feebly asleep…I knew what I had to do. I had to give back what I'd taken away. I took off the stocking that I'd put on for him, and very quickly I twisted it around his neck. He fought and thrashed…but he was too weak. As he breathed out his last breath…it slipped…warm and strong…between my lips…burned through my veins and brought the child back to life.

(*BRAND jumps up and is about to protest when ANNA holds her hand up imperiously and stops him. He sits down again.*)

(*Quietly.*) When she was born she was small and weak. I did everything I could but she became thinner and thinner and as light as a feather. I didn't want to lose her. She was so weak. I knew if she fell asleep she would never wake up. Then…one day…I was called to the bed of a young man. There had been an accident with a plough and he was bleeding. There was nothing I could do. I was holding Annie close to keep her warm. As I watched over him he breathed his last. A strong breath like a hot wind. I heard Annie give a little gasp. And when I looked at her again, she wasn't pale and thin… there were roses in her cheeks and her eyes were shining. I knew then…I knew… When she was dark and still inside me…already touched by death and cold…it was a last breath that brought her back to life. And then I knew what she needed to keep her with me. A last breath.

(*Silence.*)

BRAND: (*Appalled.*) I don't understand.

ANNA: Didn't you hear me? A last breath. (*She leans forward and blows out the candles.*)

(*The room is now much darker and only lit by the glow from the stove and the candle next to the GENERAL's bed.*)

BRAND: I don't…understand.

ANNA: (*Moves towards him with extreme agility until she seems to crouch over him.*) A…last breath! (*Breathes a slow, long breath right into his face.*)

(*BRAND averts his face.*)

(*Still crouching over him.*) My breath reeks, doesn't it? Reeks of death. Because I make my living from disease and dying. And nothing can clean me. It's part of me. My bones, my hair, my skin!

(*BRAND jumps up so suddenly that the bench falls over.*)

BRAND: Get away! Get away! Get away!

ANNA: Am I frightening you? I didn't mean to.

(*BRAND moves blindly towards the door but ANNA clings to him.*)

(*Keening in a high and terrible voice.*) Please! Please! Don't leave! I only wanted…to tell you…what she needs!

BRAND: (*Trying to throw her off.*) You vile thing! You vile, lying woman! You're insane! You're completely insane! I don't want to hear any more! (*Turns to leave.*)

ANNA: (*Gives a terrible cry.*) No!! (*Suddenly whispering urgently.*) Listen. Listen!

BRAND: What is it?

ANNA: (*Urgently.*) Oh be quiet! Listen! Can't you hear that? Can't you?

BRAND: I don't hear anything! Don't talk to me! Let go of me!

ANNA: (*Straining to listen with her head on one side.*) It's very faint. Almost just a current in the air. Something that only a mother could hear. There. There it is again. (*Pleading desperately.*) Please…please won't you go out and see? I'm so worn out. I can hardly move. It's Annie! And she's calling me! Won't you just ask her what it is? What she needs?

BRAND: I don't hear anything. What are you up to?

ANNA: Just stand near the wagon and ask her. Then come and tell me. If you're afraid…you don't have to look at her.

BRAND: Afraid of what?

ANNA: Please go and see. Just be common human decency, is that too much to ask? (*Starts weeping quietly.*) Poor little thing…she's reached the end of her strength. Tomorrow I'll bury her…in a dry river bed. I know it's the end…it's the end. (*Continues to weep.*)

BRAND: But then I'm leaving! And don't try to stop me! (*BRAND mutters then exits. Short silence. ANNA stands very still then she creeps stealthily towards the door and peers through a crack. She moves suddenly to the stove and stands, apparently warming her hands. BRAND enters. He is carrying ANNIE. She appears to be unconscious.*)

I have to bring her in. She's extremely cold. She's hardly breathing.

ANNA: Are her eyes open? (*Rushing to ANNIE.*) Her eyelids are fluttering. Thank goodness she's not quite asleep. Bring her here to the fire.

(*BRAND lays her down in front of the stove. ANNA kneels down next to her.*)

The moist night has made her clothes damp. I must get her dress off at once. Please hold her up while I unbutton her. Be quick about it!

(*BRAND crouches next to ANNIE and takes her in his arms. He holds her against him while ANNA unbuttons the dress from behind.*)

Now let me pull it off over her head. Help me. There, there.

(*ANNIE is now dressed in only a thin chemise and petticoat. Although she seemed thin in her too large dress, the delicate curves of her body are now revealed.*)

I'll blow on her feet and you blow on her hands!

(*They blow.*)

And then I want you to rub her legs like this. (*Shows him.*) To get the blood moving. I must heat a little honey. She must have some at once.

(*BRAND starts rubbing her legs slowly and rhythmically. He starts on her calves and slowly moves his hands up her thighs. Suddenly draws back as if appalled at what he is doing.*)

Don't stop.

(*BRAND continues to rub ANNIE's legs as if he's acting under a compulsion. ANNIE moans.*)

She's waking.

(*BRAND's stroking becomes slower. A deeper more sensual rhythm. ANNIE moans and then she stirs. She moves her head from side to side. She suddenly becomes aware of BRAND's presence.*)

ANNIE: It's you. (*Gives a long, voluptuous sigh.*) Your hands are so strong and warm. I'm feeling better now.

(*BRAND stops stroking. He looks at ANNIE. She lifts her arms.*)

BRAND: (*Pulling away with revulsion.*) I'm sorry. (*He averts his eyes.*)

ANNA: Why don't you lift her? Put her in the chair.

ANNIE: Please. But you must stay very near.

(*BRAND lifts her up and takes her to the chair near the fire.*)

ANNA: There. That's cosy.

ANNIE: (*Quietly to BRAND.*) And what did my mother say? Did you talk to her?

BRAND: (*Evasively.*) I talked to her.

ANNIE: And what did she say?

BRAND: Well...we'll have to see.

ANNA: Oh, you've put such a glow into her cheeks again. What a wonderful touch you have Adjutant. I must feed her this. (*Feeds her some honey.*) There. (*To BRAND.*) Well, I suppose you have to be on your way.

ANNIE: (*Very distressed.*) Are you going so soon? And will you come back?

ANNA: Of course, dear heart. Of course he'll be back. I said we'd wait for him.

ANNIE: (*Happy.*) Oh!

ANNA: Yes. He'll be away for one day and one night, that's what he told me. (*Picks up BRAND's hat.*) And don't forget your hat, Adjutant.

ANNIE: Did he?

ANNA: And he said when he comes back (*Giving the hat to BRAND.*) I hope you don't mind me telling her...he's going to take you in his arms. Press your head against his chest. Stroke your hair.

ANNIE: Oh...

ANNA: And he'll bring you a little bunch of wild flowers.

ANNIE: Oh, will you?

BRAND: Yes...

ANNIE: I'll feel it when you go away.

(*BRAND is very agitated. He is moving about restlessly, working the hat between his hands.*)

As you go...further away...my heart will grow smaller and smaller. (*Gives a cry.*) When you come back...you must stay. You must never leave again.

(*BRAND now seems very distressed. He seems desperate and confused.*)

BRAND: (*Talking to himself.*) There's a ringing in my ears and everything is dark and shadowy. I feel as if I have died and gone to hell! Will the night never end! Why is it still night? It's gone on and on and on. I've lost all sense of time. I don't know what's happened.

ANNIE: What's wrong?

ANNA: No use asking me!

BRAND: It feels like weeks, months since you stopped me on the road. But it's only been hours since I brought you here. It was getting dark then and it's still dark. (*Muttering.*) I rode off to deliver those dispatches...I came back... (*Holds his head.*) I should never have stopped for you. Never. When you ran into the road, the moon shining on your pale face...my horse shied and nearly threw me. At first I thought you were a ghost. Maybe you are.

ANNA: What a thing to say!

ANNIE: Are you angry?

BRAND: What was wrong with your wagon anyway? (*Confused.*) Why did you need my help? I can't even remember! Why can't I remember!

ANNIE: (*Distressed.*) Why are you speaking so loudly?

ANNA: (*Patiently explaining.*) The wagon was in a ditch. You helped to lift it out. And we were very grateful. I thanked you and asked if I could be of service. That's why you brought me here.

BRAND: I've never known a night like this. Just on and on and on. Hour after hour. (*Suddenly agitated.*) I must get away!

ANNA: And what about my daughter? What must I tell her? After everything you promised.

BRAND: I don't care! I must get away from here! From the pair of you!

ANNA: Well, leave at once if you want to. Nobody's stopping you. (*Makes a strange sound in the back of her throat.*)

BRAND: Why did you do that? (*Fearful.*) What does that mean? That sound.

ANNA: You poor thing. All strung up. You'll burst a vein if you're not careful.

BRAND: Oh, go to hell!

ANNA: Just please keep your voice down. We don't want to upset him do we?

BRAND: And don't you ever touch him again! (*Puts on his hat.*)

ANNA: Very well, very well. But if the wound festers...you only have yourself to blame. If the poison gets into his blood...and he dies in pain and agony...what will you do then? How will you sleep at night!

BRAND: I'm sending someone back to fetch him. The sooner the better!

ANNIE: (*To BRAND. Tearful.*) Why are you angry?

ANNA: He's not angry, my heart. Just upset and unhappy because he has to leave.

ANNIE: (*To BRAND.*) Are you angry with me?

BRAND: (*Averting his eyes.*) No.

ANNIE: Yes, you're angry. (*Starts crying softly and heart-brokenly.*) And you're never, ever coming back. I know that.

BRAND: (*Agonised.*) Please don't cry. Don't cry.

ANNA: And why shouldn't she? Let her cry. You told her you cared for her. You've broken her heart, that's what you've done. Broken her poor little heart.

(*Silence. BRAND looks utterly destroyed. The soft, broken-hearted crying continues in the silence. ANNA uses the pestle and mortar to crush herbs.*)

BRAND: (*Crouching next to ANNIE. He touches her arm.*) I'm sorry... Please don't cry... Please...

(*ANNIE continues to cry very softly with her face in her hands. BRAND watches her helplessly. Suddenly he gives a low moan, then he puts his arms around her.*)

Stop crying... (*Brokenly.*) I'll be back.

ANNIE: (*Stops crying.*) Oh...I thought I'd die.

BRAND: Don't talk. Don't talk. You have to rest.

ANNA: Yes. Don't waste your breath on him.

ANNIE: He's coming back. He promised.

ANNA: Really?

BRAND: Yes.

ANNA: Well, everything's all right then. (*To ANNIE.*) You
upset yourself for nothing. (*Goes to BRAND.*) I'm deeply
moved. You are a gentleman after all. A man of your word.
You've made my Annie very happy. This is a great day for
me. A great day. I've waited so long. Waited and hoped.
(*ANNIE looks very happy.*)
We have to have a celebration! (*To BRAND.*) I'm sure you
don't have to leave this minute! (*Rushes to the trunk.*) I have
just the thing! (*Produces two glasses and a half-bottle of wine.*)
Look! A little sweet wine. (*To BRAND.*) Help her up. We'll
sit near the stove. You can hold her on your lap, if you
want to. You're allowed to do that now. (*Laughs. Pours some
wine into the glasses. She pours only a little wine into her own
glass, but fills up the other and adds a pinch of fine herbs.*)
(*BRAND takes off his hat and puts it on the table. He lifts
ANNIE. He sits on the chair and pulls her onto his lap. She
nestles against his chest.*)

ANNIE: (*Giggles.*) I can smell your horse.

BRAND: I'm sorry. I'm not very clean.

ANNIE: And…your skin. (*Sighs with pleasure.*)

ANNA: (*Giving BRAND the glass.*) There you are. She can also
have a little. But only the smallest drop. (*Sits down on the
stool. Raises her glass.*) Let's drink to a safe journey.

ANNIE: A safe journey.
(*BRAND drinks deeply.*)
And what about me?

BRAND: I'm sorry. (*Gives her a sip from his glass.*)

ANNA: Soon…the two of you will be sleeping in the wagon at
night. I'll be holding the reins and keeping my eyes on the
road. I know what's right and fitting. And if you hold her
very lightly…she'll never get away again.
(*ANNA and BRAND drink.*)
But you'll have to…be patient and gentle… She's never
ever seen a man before

ANNIE: But I have!

ANNA: I mean, without his clothes on. Oh, except for that
one time. A man was swimming in a stream. When he got
out on the other side he was stark naked.

179

ANNIE: Wet and covered in slime.

ANNA: I clapped my hand over her eyes and said, 'Don't look.' Just in time.

ANNA: Give me your glass. We might as well have it all. This doesn't happen every day. (*Fills his glass.*)

(*BRAND drinks as ANNA continues to speak. He looks slightly dazed.*)

I want you to know… I've raised her like a lady. Because we travel in a wagon…doesn't mean we're not…people of quality. We come from a very old family. And she knows all about the fine things. Only the softest muslin against her skin and washed with perfumed soap. Her hair is always soft and clean.

(*ANNIE suddenly gives a loud, terrible cry of pain and doubles up.*)

BRAND: What is it?

ANNA: My poor little girl! (*Aside to BRAND.*) It's the pain. It's begun. It won't be very long now.

(*As the scene continues, ANNIE whimpers, moans and sometimes screams. She is obviously in terrible, almost unbearable pain.*)

BRAND: Oh God…is there nothing we can do?

ANNA: (*Weeps.*) Just hold her tightly. Let her know you're here.

(*BRAND holds ANNIE tightly as she writhes in pain.*)

BRAND: I'm here…I'm here.

ANNA: It's tearing her apart. Ah…ah… (*Wails softly.*) Her small bones…her soft and tender heart. Ah…

BRAND: (*Strokes ANNIE's hair as she convulses in pain. Suddenly crying out. In deep distress.*) I can't see her like this!

ANNA: (*Bitterly.*) Well, lay her down on the floor. Lay her down. Let me tend to her.

(*BRAND gets up and lays her down on the floor. He turns away. After two glasses of wine on a very empty stomach, he seems unsteady on his feet.*)

(*Crouching next to ANNIE.*) My little heart. I won't leave you. (*To BRAND.*) Go, then! Go! Run away! That's all you're good for. All of you!

(*BRAND stumbles to the door. He opens it and exits. ANNIE gives a low scream which rises to a terrible, almost animal intensity. BRAND appears in the door again. He seems completely distraught. Loud gusts of wind can be heard coming through the open door.)*

BRAND: (*Beside himself.*) Do something… We must…do something… We must… Make her stop!!
(ANNA gets up, moves quickly to him. She grips his upper arms and shakes him.)

ANNA: Be quiet! Be quiet!
(BRAND calms down a little.)
There is something we can do. I've told you, haven't I? In a moment it could all be over. All her pain and suffering.
(ANNA draws in her breath. Then she breathes out very slowly, looking fixedly at BRAND.)
(BRAND looks at her without speaking. He is breathing in gasps. He is in a state of shock. ANNIE gives a broken cry.)

BRAND: (*Fearfully.*) What…are you trying to say?
(ANNA stares at him fixedly then turns her head and looks at the GENERAL. BRAND gasps and steps back.)

ANNA: We'll be helping him really. Putting him out of his misery. Better sooner than later. Just see how he's suffering. Yes, he's probably done for anyway. Poor thing.

BRAND: You're insane, and that's the truth. You're completely bloody insane!

ANNA: Be quiet. You'll wake him.

BRAND: (*Holding his head.*) Stay away from him. Over my dead body!

ANNA: (*With extreme bitterness.*) Don't get so excited. It was only a thought. But…I can see…it's no use. No use. Oh!
(Suddenly gives a wail of agony and tears the bodice of her dress. She exposes more of her breasts and part of her chemise.)

BRAND: What are you doing!

ANNA: (*Frantically starts looking for something.*) And when I find the small scissors, I'll cut off my hair to the roots! And then I'll smear the ash from the stove all over my face!
(ANNIE gives a high and repetitive cry.)
And please…you will have to bury her. I won't have any strength left. Please…I beg you. A proper grave, and deep. So no wild animals will find her. (*Picks up the shovel and*

holds it out to him.) You might as well start now. No point in waiting.

BRAND: Do it then! Do what you must do! I can't take it any more! I'd rather be dammed!

ANNA: Oh, thank you. Thank you. I knew you'd understand, I knew it.

BRAND: But I don't want to know. I…don't want to see.
(*Stumbles towards the door.*)

ANNA: Excuse me!
(*BRAND turns around.*)
Excuse me, my dear Adjutant Brand. You don't seem to understand…that I need your help. I know it's…difficult …but I do.
(*A shiver passes through BRAND. ANNIE moans and whimpers.*)
(*Going to ANNIE.*) Help me, Adjutant. We must lift her and take her over there. (*Points to the GENERAL.*) Put her as near the General as you can.

BRAND: I…

ANNA: I won't be able to do it on my own. I'm getting on you know. What can you expect?
(*BRAND lifts ANNIE and carries her to the GENERAL.*)

BRAND: Where must I put her?

ANNA: Put her next to him. On the floor. (*Picks up the shawl.*)
(*BRAND puts ANNIE down next to the GENERAL.*)

ANNIE: (*With her arms around his neck.*) I wish…you could carry me…far away from here.

BRAND: Yes.

ANNA: (*Giving the shawl to BRAND.*) Put this under her head.
(*BRAND puts the shawl under ANNIE's head. ANNA moves away again and moves to the trunk. She starts rummaging through the trunk.*)

ANNIE: (*Grabbing BRAND's arm urgently.*) You must leave! Please! (*Closes her eyes and moans.*)
(*ANNA turns around. She is holding a silk stocking, stretching and twisting it between her hands.*)

ANNA: He mustn't wake up. Much better that way. For him and for me. I'm old and feeble now. I can only strangle a man in his sleep. Even if you hold his feet, it's too difficult

for me. (*Going towards the GENERAL.*) So we have to hope
for the best.

BRAND: (*Getting up.*) I have to get out of here. (*Stumbles
blindly towards the door.*)

ANNIE: Yes. Go!

ANNA: But excuse me, Adjutant. Didn't you hear me. I
thought I spoke quite clearly. I told you that I needed you.

BRAND: (*Desperate.*) For what? For what do you need me?

ANNA: Obviously, to hold his feet. To hold his feet very
firmly. So that he doesn't thrash about. (*Taking a frayed rope
out of a concealed pocket in her dress.*) I'll tie his hands. But if
he thrashes around with his legs...I won't manage. Even
when they are asleep...they wake up at the end. (*Starts
tying the GENERAL's wrists together.*) Don't just sit there.
Hold his feet. Or sit on his lap. You can look the other way.
You're wasting time!

(*ANNIE is whimpering softly and brokenly. BRAND approaches
the GENERAL slowly and with great trepidation.*)

(*Tying the knot.*) There. That should hold. Come on!

(*BRAND closes his eyes, he leans forward and presses down on
the GENERAL's legs. The GENERAL moans and mutters.
ANNA goes to stand behind the GENERAL. She is twisting
the silk stocking between her hands.*)

(*To BRAND.*) Don't let go, whatever you do. (*To ANNIE.*)
Come, my girl. Turn your head to the side and open your
nostrils very wide. Be ready when I say 'now'.

BRAND: (*Suddenly breaks away. Moans. Bends forward and holds
his head. Tonelessly, under his breath.*) I must be mad.
I must...be mad. I...must...be mad... (*Loudly.*) I must be
mad!

(*ANNIE is still whimpering softly.*)

ANNA: (*Speaking ovr his muttering.*) Have it your own way!
(*With deep desperation.*) I'm tired. I can't go on any more.
(*Picks up the shovel again.*) Out there...under the pepper tree.
It's a good place. And...make it deep...as I've said. (*She
sinks down on her straw bed.*) There's...nothing more I can
do. (*Closes her eyes as if she's fainting.*)

ANNIE: Where...are you? Where are you?

(*BRAND crouches next to ANNIE.*)
Is…that…you?

BRAND: Yes.

ANNIE: Hold me. Hold me close. (*Gives a terrible, prolonged, barely human cry of agony.*)

BRAND: (*To ANNA.*) Stop this! Do something!
(*ANNA doesn't respond.*)
Do something!! Do something!! (*Rushes to ANNA.*) Wake up! (*He shakes her.*) Wake up you stupid bitch!!
(*ANNIE's cries, lower now, continue until otherwise indicated in the text.*)
(*Slaps her.*) Wake up!

ANNA: (*Weakly, opening her eyes.*) Are you speaking to me?

BRAND: Don't leave me with her! Do something!

ANNA: There's only one thing to do. I've told you, haven't I?

BRAND: I've served him… Given him everything. All these years… We all…follow him! All of us! The men… Our… country! (*Rushes to his gun and picks it up beside himself.*) You can have me! I'll shoot myself! (*Frantic.*) I want it to be over and done with! I want it to be… finished!

ANNA: Wait! It won't do any good! A violent, sudden death is no use at all. It's too fast… The last breath must come out slowly. A…long breath. Strangling is the best. Or bleeding… Growing weaker and weaker. But there's no time for that.

BRAND: (*Shouting.*) Well, strangle me then! Strangle me, you murdering bitch!

ANNA: You're so kind. You overwhelm me. But who's going to hold your legs? When you start choking your legs will be kicking. I'll have to tie you up.

BRAND: Do what you must! Just get it over with!

ANNA: (*Takes him by the arm and leads him to the armchair. She pushes him down.*) Sit there!
(*BRAND sits.*)
(*Lifts her skirt and takes two thick pieces of thong from a secret pocket in her petticoat.*) Give me your hands.
(*BRAND suddenly draws back and seems afraid.*)

ANNIE: (*Turning her head to ANNA.*) No! Don't hurt him! No!
I...beg you. Don't hurt him!

ANNA: He wants to, my girl. He cares for you more than for
his own life!

ANNIE: (*Reaches out her hand towards BRAND.*) No... No...
(*Cries bitterly.*)
(*BRAND seems defeated and a little dazed.*)

ANNA: (*Deftly tying his hands behind his back.*) Poor little thing.
She would spare you if she could. (*Quickly moves to his feet.
To ANNIE.*) Stop crying my girl. This is what he wants to
do. He wants you to be strong and healthy. (*Ties his ankles
together and winds the thong around the legs of the chair.*) To run
and dance under the stars. (*Stretches the thong and ties it deftly
around the back of the chair.*) Your name will always be on
her lips. And she will keep you in her heart.
(*BRAND is now immobilised.*)
(*Standing up with her hands pressed to the small of her back.*)
There we are! My poor back. It gets harder and harder
every time.
(*ANNIE falls ominously silent. ANNA suddenly seems older and
frail. She moves with difficulty towards the stove.*)
(*Weakly.*) I...must sit down...for a little while. My poor
bones...feel as heavy...and cold...as stones. (*Sits down
heavily.*) At least now...I can take my time. (*Sighs deeply.*)
(*BRAND realises that he is completely powerless.*)

BRAND: I don't think...I want to do this. I would if I could...
But...I have...important business.
(*ANNA yawns vastly and falls silent.*)
(*Straining against the thongs.*) More...dispatches... Attacks...
to be planned. I'm expected you see... My men...are
waiting for me. I don't...have time to waste like this.

ANNA: (*Sympathetically.*) I wish...I wish I could let you go.
I know you're an important man. And very busy. (*Sighs.*)
But unfortunately I can't. You see...I need you. It's for my
daughter, you understand. But don't worry. It won't be
long now. I only...have to rest for a while. I've had such a
hard day.

BRAND: There's a war out there! And they need me! Let me
go! I'm ordering you!

ANNA: (*Rises and stretches.*) Now I feel refreshed. And quite
strong enough. (*Takes the stocking from the pocket in her dress.
Starts stretching and twisting it between her hands.*)

BRAND: (*Thrashing about.*) You murdering bitch! Let me go!
They'll hang you! From the nearest tree!

ANNA: (*Moving towards him.*) If you go quietly it will be much
easier. Believe me, I know.

BRAND: (*Making sounds of extreme fear.*) Stay away! Stay away!

ANNA: (*Soothingly.*) Come now. Soon it will all be over. Soon.
Soon.

BRAND: Take *him* then! Take him! That's what you want me
to say, isn't it? Well, take him then! He's half dead anyway.
Take *him*!

ANNA: (*Explaining, as if to a child.*) I never...wanted him.

BRAND: (*Shocked into silence. Fearfully.*) What do you mean?

ANNA: He's no good. So sick and close to death. No, no that
won't do. We need...a good...strong...breath.

BRAND: (*With horror.*) So...it was always me? You wanted *me*.
From the beginning.

(*ANNA smiles down at him.*)

Did *she* know? (*Twists around and looks at ANNIE.*)

(*ANNIE sits quite still staring at him.*)

(*To ANNIE. Fearful.*) Why...are you...so quiet? Why...so
quiet?

ANNA: She knew, didn't you my girl?

ANNIE: (*Turns her face away.*) I told you...to leave this place. I
told you. But you mustn't be scared. Everything will be all
right.

BRAND: You knew!

ANNIE: (*Softly.*) Yes. I knew. (*Lowers her eyes demurely.*) I'm
very, very sorry.

BRAND: You bitches from hell! You trapped me! Tricked me!

ANNA: (*Standing behind him.*) She was really fond of you.
Truly. I could see it plainly.

ANNIE: It's true! It's true!

ANNA: She cared more for you than for any of the others.
Believe me.

(*BRAND makes sounds of terror. He struggles to get free.*)

Let that be a comfort to you.

BRAND: Help me! Help! General! Wake up! General! Help me!

GENERAL: (*Opens his eyes.*) Who's that?

BRAND: (*Frantic.*) Help! Help!!

GENERAL: Who's there? Speak, man! Never surrender! (*His eyes close and he breathes heavily and raspingly.*)

(*As BRAND continues to speak in incoherent snatches, half crazed with terror, ANNIE crawls towards him. When she reaches the chair, she climbs on top of him, her hands on the back of the chair.*)

ANNIE: Wait! Please, please do this because you want to. For me! Then we'll be happy, I promise.

BRAND: Get away!

ANNIE: Please! I promise! (*A desperate cry.*) Why won't you believe me!!

BRAND: You vile thing! Get off me!

ANNA: (*Softly.*) It's no use. You see, my girl? Now, are you ready?

(*ANNIE nods. ANNA twists the stocking around BRAND's neck. ANNIE leans forward. Her long hair covers his face. BRAND writhes and makes strangling sounds. The thrashing becomes weaker. As soon as he is still, the sound of a loud, long last breath being exhaled while ANNIE breathes in deeply. She moans. She shudders, then lies quietly with her head on BRAND's chest.*)

(*ANNA leans forward and strokes ANNIE's hair tenderly, crooning.*) There...there... All better now. All...better. (*She closes BRAND's eyes and turns his head to the side.*) Open... your eyes.

(*ANNIE lifts her head slightly.*)

(*Staggering slightly.*) Oh...how it's taken it out of me. I'm quite dizzy. (*Steadies herself. Stretches out her hands.*) Come, my girl. You must get up. I'll help you.

(*ANNIE sits up slowly.*)

And don't look at him. It will only upset you.

ANNIE: (*Stretching out her arms.*) I won't.

(*ANNA helps ANNIE out of the chair.*)

ANNA: Oh...look at you! So steady on your feet. Come and take my arm. Try to walk a little.

(*ANNIE takes her arm as they walk slowly towards the bench near the stove. They sit down.*)

Oh… (*Long sigh of pleasure.*) I can see the colour coming into your cheeks. Just a first little flush. But it tells me that hot, strong blood is rushing through your veins! Soon you'll be yourself again. Soon. (*Laughs.*) But why aren't you happy, my little girl? Why that sadness in your eyes.

ANNIE: Oh…I liked him very much. Very…very much. (*She wrings her hands.*) My heart aches.

ANNA: You poor little thing.

ANNIE: It hurts. (*Presses her palm against her heart.*)

ANNA: (*Tenderly.*) It will get better. You'll see.

(*ANNIE touches the locket and then looks at it.*)

You can't keep that.

ANNIE: Why?

ANNA: (*Explaining patiently.*) Because *he* gave it to you. It will only remind you.

(*ANNIE sighs sadly. She opens the locket. She takes out the hair. She holds it between her fingers. Then she blows softly. She opens her fingers and the hair is blown into the air.*)

There now.

(*Sadly ANNIE takes off the locket and puts it on the crate. ANNA and ANNIE sit in silence for a time. They stare out front and look forlorn. Only the dim glow from the stove lights up their faces. Dry gusts of wind rattle the door and the GENERAL's laboured breathing can still be heard.*)

(*Quietly and sadly.*) I hoped it was him. After all he was a handsome young man. And the youngest of three. I even…imagined that I…recognised his face. There was a moment. In the candlelight. And something in his voice… And…words that he spoke. (*With infinite sorrow.*) Him. The one I keep seeing in my dreams. I wanted it to be.

ANNIE: But it never is! (*She starts weeping softly and her head drops onto ANNA's shoulder.*)

ANNA: The poor young man. He didn't believe you. He knew about war and honour but he didn't know you, my girl. He didn't know your pure and simple heart.

ANNIE: What a pity! All the fighting and struggling…and where did that get him?

ANNA: (*Tenderly stroking her hair.*) Don't cry. Don't cry. One day…it will be. You'll see. One day he'll suddenly be there. Suddenly. Appearing out of nowhere. Believe me, my girl. One day he'll be there. (*Short silence. Musingly.*) A good man.

ANNIE: (*Quietly. Echoing.*) Good.

ANNA: Who never breaks his promises.

ANNIE: Never ever.

ANNA: With a strong heart.

ANNIE: A strong heart.

ANNA: He won't be frightened…of anything.

ANNIE: Of nothing.

ANNA: We won't have to lie. Or tie him up.

ANNIE: We won't.

ANNA: Because…when I ask him…he'll *want* to.

ANNIE: Yes…

ANNA: To…breathe his strong life into you.
(*ANNIE sighs with longing.*)
You'll draw it in. So deep. So deep.

ANNIE: So…burning.

ANNA: Oh, the pleasure of it. It will make you…sigh.
(*ANNIE sighs.*)
So sweet. So sweet. And that sigh…will slip…between his open lips… Each giving what the other takes… At that moment… At that very moment.

ANNIE: Our eyes will also close.

ANNA: And we'll sleep. Sleep. Sleep.

ANNIE: And…dream.

ANNA/ANNIE: (*Together.*) Dream…the same dream.
(*Short silence. They are transported.*)

ANNIE: An open field…

ANNA: Under a clear sky…

ANNIE: And…the warm air…smelling of seedgrass…and honey. And *he* will be there. I'll go to him and lay my head on his breast.
(*They both sigh. Silence. They look out front, enraptured.*)

ANNA: Like a small homing bird that's found its nest.

ANNIE: Yes…

(*Short silence. They both look transported.*)

ANNA: And then I'll sing you my song. I've waited such
a long time to sing my song. (*Suddenly animated. Slightly
forced.*) But…in the meantime…we'll manage. We always
have, haven't we?

ANNIE: Yes.

ANNA: (*Jumping up.*) Enough of this! Come now! We must be
happy! Look at you! Your lips are red as cherries! How do
you feel, my girl?

(*ANNIE gets up carefully and takes a few tentative steps. Then
she moves more boldly and starts turning with out-stretched
arms.*)

ANNIE: (*Laughing and turning.*) I feel so light. So light.

ANNA: (*Laughing.*) Just look at you!

ANNIE: (*Leaning against the table.*) I'm dizzy. But I don't want
to stop!

ANNA: Why don't you go outside my girl. Get some fresh air.

ANNIE: Yes! Yes! I want to go outside. (*Moves to the door.*)

ANNA: I think the moon is setting, but there's still some
light. Then I'll pack up here and soon we'll be back in our
wagon.

ANNIE: (*Looking out.*) The stars…the stars.

ANNA: Wait! You must put on your shoes. There are sharp
stones and thorns.

(*ANNIE runs gaily to the trunk and finds a pair of red shoes.
She sits on the table and puts the shoes on.*)

And don't be too long. You know we must leave before
dawn.

ANNIE: (*Jumps up from the table.*) I know! (*Runs out.*)

(*ANNA shakes her head as she smiles and clicks her tongue
fondly. Then she gets up and with extreme economy of movement,
she packs the mortar and pestle, the bowl and jug, the knife, the
candles and the rest of her belongings. She blows out the candle
next to the GENERAL's bed and packs it as well. The shed is
now lit only by the shadowy moonlight coming through the open
door and the dim glow from the embers in the stove. She slams
the lid of the trunk shut and staggering under its weight, puts
it outside the door. She straightens up and looks out into the*

distance. *She shakes her head and chuckles fondly. She cups her hands around her mouth.*)

ANNA: (*Calling loudly.*) Yes, my girl! Run! Run! It will make you strong!

(*ANNA turns back, picks up the green chair quite easily with one hand and puts it outside. She enters again and goes to BRAND. She looks at him for a moment and then starts untying the thongs. While she does this she slowly whisper-sings with infinite sadness.*)

How do you go to your love

On the wings of the night wind?

Which road leads to your love?

All the roads in the world.

(*Brokenly.*) All…the…roads…in the…world.

GENERAL: (*Mumbling.*) To…the last man. Never surrender…

(*Continues to mumble softly.*)

(*ANNA leans forward, untwists the stocking from around BRAND's neck and slips it into a small pocket in the skirt of her dress. She moves away but suddenly stops as if remembering something. She turns, goes back to BRAND and starts pulling his boots off. She pulls the boots off both his feet at once. She pulls and tugs and when the boots come off, BRAND's feet thud dully onto the floor. She then takes the gun off the hook and slings it over her shoulder. After a moment's hesitation she picks up BRAND's hat and puts it on. ANNA exits rapidly without looking back. A moment later she re-appears. She is standing outside the door. Her hands are empty now. For moments she looks, with an inscrutable gaze, into the dim interior of the shed. Then she raises her arms and pushes the door shut. It shuts noiselessly. The interior is now very dimly lit and the two prone figures are hardly discernable.*)

Ne…ver…sur…ren…der.

(*He starts breathing in a very laboured way.*)

(*Only the slow, laboured breathing of the GENERAL can be heard as the lights fade slowly to black.*)